AMONG THE FARMYARD PEOPLE

Look for these other great books by Clara Dillingham Pierson also from Living Book Press

- Among the Farmyard People
- Among the Pond People
- Among the Forest People
- Among the Meadow People
- Among the Night People
- Dooryard Stories
- Tales from a Poultry Farm

WWW.LIVINGBOOKPRESS.COM

This edition published 2021
by Living Book Press
Copyright © Living Book Press, 2021

ISBN: 978-1-922634-15-3 (hardcover)
       978-1-922634-14-6 (softcover)

First published in 1899.

All rights reserved. No part of this publication may be reproduced, stored in a retrieval system, or transmitted in any other form or means – electronic, mechanical, photocopying, recording or otherwise, without the prior permission of the copyright owner and the publisher or as provided by Australian law.

A catalogue record for this book is available from the National Library of Australia

Among the Farmyard People

BY

CLARA DILLINGHAM PIERSON

TO THE CHILDREN

Dear Little Friends:

I want to introduce the farmyard people to you, and to have you call upon them and become better acquainted as soon as you can. Some of them are working for us, and we surely should know them. Perhaps, too, some of us are working for them, since that is the way in this delightful world of ours, and one of the happiest parts of life is helping and being helped.

It is so in the farmyard, and although there is not much work that the people there can do for each other, there are many kind things to be said, and even the Lame Duckling found that he could make the Blind Horse happy when he tried. It is there as it is everywhere else, and I sometimes think that although the farmyard people do not look like us or talk like us, they are not so very different after all. If you had seen the little Chicken who wouldn't eat gravel when his mother was reproving him, you could not have helped knowing his thoughts even if you did not understand a word of the Chicken language. He was thinking, "I don't care! I don't care a bit! So now!" That was long since, for he was a Chicken when I was a little girl, and both of us grew up some time ago. I think I have always been more sorry for him because when he was learning to eat gravel I was learning to eat some things which I did not like; and so, you see, I knew exactly how he felt. But it was not until afterwards that I found out how his mother felt.

That is one of the stories which I have been keeping a long time for you, and the Chicken was a particular friend of mine. I knew him better than I did some of his neighbors; yet they were all pleasant acquaintances, and if I did not see some of these things happen with my own eyes, it is just because I was not in the farmyard at the right time. There are many other tales I should like to tell you about them, but one mustn't make the book too fat and heavy for your hands to hold, so I will send you these and keep the rest.

Many stories might be told about our neighbors who live out-of-doors, and they are stories that ought to be told, too, for there are still boys and girls who do not know that animals think and talk and work, and love their babies, and help each other when in trouble. I knew one boy who really thought it was not wrong to steal newly built birds'-nests, and I have seen girls—quite large ones, too—who were afraid of Mice! It was only last winter that a Quail came to my front door, during the very cold weather, and snuggled down into the warmest corner he could find. I fed him, and he stayed there for several days, and I know, and you know, perfectly well that although he did not say it in so many words, he came to remind me that I had not yet told you a Quail story. And two of my little neighbors brought ten Polliwogs to spend the day with me, so I promised then and there that the next book should be about pond people and have a Polliwog story in it.

And now, good-bye! Perhaps some of you will write

me about your visits to the farmyard. I hope you will enjoy them very much, but be sure you don't wear red dresses or caps when you call on the Turkey Gobbler.

    Your friend,

               CLARA DILLINGHAM PIERSON.

            STANTON, MICHIGAN, *March 28, 1899.*

CONTENTS

THE STORY THAT THE SWALLOW DIDN'T TELL	1
THE LAMB WITH THE LONGEST TAIL	8
THE WONDERFUL SHINY EGG	14
THE DUCKLING WHO DIDN'T KNOW WHAT TO DO	21
THE FUSSY QUEEN BEE	30
THE BAY COLT LEARNS TO MIND	39
THE TWIN LAMBS	50
THE VERY SHORT STORY OF THE FOOLISH LITTLE MOUSE	58
THE LONELY LITTLE PIG	64
THE KITTEN WHO LOST HERSELF	71
THE CHICKEN WHO WOULDN'T EAT GRAVEL	83
THE GOOSE WHO WANTED HER OWN WAY	90
WHY THE SHEEP RAN AWAY	97
THE FINE YOUNG RAT AND THE TRAP	104
THE QUICK-TEMPERED TURKEY GOBBLER	112
THE BRAGGING PEACOCK	120
THE DISCONTENTED GUINEA HEN	129
THE OXEN TALK WITH THE CALVES	139

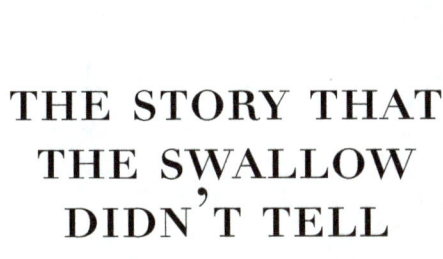

THE STORY THAT THE SWALLOW DIDN'T TELL

"Listen!" said the Nigh Ox, "don't you hear some friends coming?"

The Off Ox raised his head from the grass and stopped to brush away a Fly, for you never could hurry either of the brothers. "I don't hear any footfalls," said he.

"You should listen for wings, not feet," said the Nigh Ox, "and for voices, too."

Even as he spoke there floated down from the clear air overhead a soft "tittle-ittle-ittle-ee," as though some bird were laughing for happiness. There was not a cloud in the sky, and the meadow was covered with thousands and thousands of green grass blades, each so small and tender, and yet together making a most beautiful carpet for the feet of the farmyard people, and offering them sweet and juicy food after their winter fare of hay and grain. Truly it was a day to make one laugh aloud for joy. The alder tassels fluttered and danced in the spring breeze, while the smallest and shyest of the willow pussies crept from their little brown houses on the branches to grow in the sunshine.

"Tittle-ittle-ittle-ee! Tittle-ittle-ittle-ee!" And this time it was louder and clearer than before.

"The Swallows!" cried the Oxen to each other. Then they straightened their strong necks and bellowed to the Horses, who were drawing the plow in the field beyond, "The Swallows are coming!"

As soon as the Horses reached the end of the furrow and could rest a minute, they tossed their heads and whinnied with delight. Then they looked around at the farmer, and wished that he knew enough of the farmyard language to understand what they wanted to tell him. They knew he would be glad to hear of their friends' return, for had they not seen him pick up a young Swallow one day and put him in a safer place?

"Tittle-ittle-ittle-ee!" and there was a sudden darkening of the sky above their heads, a whirr of many wings, a chattering and laughing of soft voices, and the Swallows had come. Perched on the ridge-pole of the big barn, they rested and visited and heard all the news.

The Doves were there, walking up and down the sloping sides of the roof and cooing to each other about the simple things of every-day life. You know the Doves stay at home all winter, and so it makes a great change when their neighbors, the Swallows, return. They are firm friends in spite of their very different ways of living. There was never a Dove who would be a Swallow if he could, yet the plump, quiet, gray and white Doves dearly love the dashing Swallows, and happy is the Squab who can get a Swallow to tell him stories of the great world.

"Isn't it good to be home, home, home!" sang one Swallow. "I never set my claws on another ridge-pole as comfortable as this."

"I'm going to look at my old nest," said a young Swallow, as she suddenly flew down to the eaves.

"I think I'll go, too," said another young Swallow, springing away from his perch. He was a handsome fellow, with a glistening dark blue head and back, a long forked tail which showed a white stripe on the under side, a rich buff vest, and a deep blue collar, all of the finest feathers. He loved the young Swallow whom he was following, and he wanted to tell her so.

"There is the nest where I was hatched," she said. "Would you think I was ever crowded in there with five brothers and sisters? It was a comfortable nest, too, before the winter winds and snow wore it away. I wonder how it would seem to be a fledgling again?" She snuggled down in the old nest until he could see only her forked tail and her dainty head over the edge. Her vest was quite hidden, and the only light feathers that showed were the reddish-buff ones on throat and face; these were not so bright as his, but still she was beautiful to him. He loved every feather on her body.

"I don't want you to be a fledgling again," he cried. "I want you to help me make a home under the eaves, a lovely little nest of mud and straw, where you can rest as you are now doing, while I bring food to you. Will you?"

"Yes," she cried. "Tittle-ittle-ittle-ee! Oh, tittle-ittle-ittle-ee!" And she flew far up into the blue sky, while he followed her, twittering and singing.

"Where are those young people going?" said an older Swallow. "I should think they had flown far enough for to-day without circling around for the fun of it."

"Don't you remember the days when you were young?" said the Swallow next to him.

"When I was young?" he answered. "My dear, I am young now. I shall always be young in the springtime. I shall never be old except when I am moulting."

Just then a family of Doves came pattering over the roof, swaying their heads at every step. "We are so glad to see you back," said the father. "We had a long, cold winter, and we thought often of you."

"A very cold winter," cooed his plump little wife.

"Tell me a story," said a young Dove, their son.

"Hush, hush," said the Father Dove. "This is our son," he added, "and this is his sister. We think them quite a pair. Our last brood, you know."

"Tell us a story," said the young Dove again.

"Hush, dear. You mustn't tease the Swallow," said his mother. "They are so fond of stories," she cooed, "and they have heard that your family are great travellers."

"But I want him to tell us a story," said the young Dove. "I think he might."

This made the Swallow feel very uncomfortable, for he could see that the children had been badly brought up, and he did not want to tell a story just then.

"Perhaps you would like to hear about our journey south," said he. "Last fall, when the maples began to show red and yellow leaves among the green, we felt like flying away. It was quite warm weather, and the forest birds were still here, but when we feel like flying south we always begin to get ready."

"I never feel like flying south," said the young Dove. "I don't see why you should."

"That is because I am a Swallow and you are a farmyard Dove. We talked about it to each other, and one day we were ready to start. We all had on our new feathers and felt strong and well. We started out together, but the young birds and their mothers could not keep up with the rest, so we went on ahead."

"Ahead of whom?" said the young Dove, who had been preening his feathers when he should have been listening.

"Ahead of the mothers and their fledglings. We flew over farms where there were Doves like you; over rivers where the Wild Ducks were feeding by the shore; and over towns where crowds of boys and girls were going into large buildings, while on top of these buildings were large bells singing, 'Ding dong, ding dong, ding dong.'"

"I don't think that was a very pretty song," said the young Dove.

"Hush," said his mother, "you mustn't interrupt the Swallow."

"And at last we came to a great lake," said the Swallow. "It was so great that when we had flown over it for a little while we could not see land at all, and our eyes would not tell us which way to go. We just went on as birds must in such places, flying as we felt we ought, and not stopping to ask why or to wonder if we were right. Of course we Swallows never stop to eat, for we catch our food as we fly, but we did sometimes stop to rest. Just after we had crossed this great lake we alighted. It was then that a very queer thing happened, and this is really the story that I started to tell."

"Oh!" said the young Dove and his sister. "How very exciting. But wait just a minute while we peep over the edge of the roof and see what the farmer is doing." And before anybody could say a word they had pattered away to look.

The birds who were there say that the Swallow seemed quite disgusted, and surely nobody could blame him if he did.

"You must excuse them," cooed their mother. "They are really hardly more than Squabs yet, and I can't bear to speak severely to them. I'm sure they didn't mean to be rude."

"Certainly, certainly," said the Swallow. "I will excuse them and you must excuse me. I wish to see a few of my old friends before the sun goes down. Good afternoon!" And he darted away.

The young Doves came pattering back, swaying their heads as they walked. "Why, where is the Swallow?" they cried. "What made him go away? Right at the best part of the story, too. We don't see why folks are so disagreeable. People never are as nice to us as they are to the other young Doves."

"Hush," said their mother. "You mustn't talk in that way. Fly off for something to eat, and never mind about the rest of the story."

When they were gone, she said to her husband, "I wonder if they did hurt the Swallow's feelings? But then, they are so young, hardly more than Squabs."

She forgot that even Squabs should be thoughtful of others, and that no Dove ever amounts to anything unless he begins in the right way as a Squab.

THE LAMB WITH THE LONGEST TAIL

THE Sheep are a simple and kind-hearted family, and of all the people on the farm there are none who are more loved than they. All summer they wander in the fields, nibbling the fresh, sweet grass, and resting at noon in the shadow of the trees, but when the cold weather comes they are brought up to the farmyard and make their home in the long low Sheep-shed.

That is always a happy time. The Horses breathe deeply and toss their heads for joy, the Cows say to each other, "Glad to have the Sheep come up," and even the Oxen shift their cuds and look long over their shoulders at the woolly newcomers. And this is not because the Sheep can do anything for their neighbors to make them warm or to feed them. It is only because they are a gentle folk and pleasant in all they say; and you know when people are always kind, it makes others happy just to see them and have them near.

Then, when the cold March winds are blowing, the good farmer brings more yellow straw into the Sheep-shed, and sees that it is warm and snug. If there are any boards broken and letting the wind in, he mends them and shuts out the cold. At this time, too, the Horses and Cattle stop often in their eating to listen. Even the Pigs, who do not think much about their neighbors, root in the corners nearest the Sheep-shed and prick up their ears.

Some bleak morning they hear a faint bleating and know

that the first Lamb is there. And then from day to day they hear more of the soft voices as the new Lambs come to live with the flock. Such queer little creatures as the Lambs are when they first come—so weak and awkward! They can hardly stand alone, and stagger and wobble around the little rooms or pens where they are with their mothers. You can just imagine how hard it must be to learn to manage four legs all at once!

There is one thing which they do learn very quickly, and that is, to eat. They are hungry little people, and well they may be, for they have much growing to do, and all of the food that is to be made into good stout bodies and fine long wool has to go into their mouths and down their throats to their stomachs. It is very wonderful to think that a Cow eats grass and it is turned into hair to keep her warm, a Goose eats grass and grows feathers, and a Sheep eats grass and grows wool. Still, it is so, and nobody in the world can tell why. It is just one of the things that are, and if you should ask "Why?" nobody could tell you the reason. There are many such things which we cannot understand, but there are many more which we can, so it would be very foolish for us to mind when there is no answer to our "Why?"

Yes, Sheep eat grass, and because they have such tiny mouths they have to take small mouthfuls. The Lambs have different food for a while,—warm milk from their mothers' bodies. When a mother has a Lamb to feed, she eats a great deal, hay, grass, and chopped turnips, and then part of the food that goes into her stomach is turned into milk and stored in two warm bags for the Lamb to take when he is hungry. And how the Lambs do like this milk! It tastes so good that they can hardly stand still while they drink it down, and they give funny little jerks and wave their woolly tails in the air.

There was one Lamb who had a longer tail than any of the rest, and, sad to say, it made him rather vain. When he first came, he was too busy drinking milk and learning to walk, to think about tails, but as he grew older and stronger he began to know that he had the longest one. Because he was a very young Lamb he was so foolish as to tease the others and call out, "Baa! your tails are snippy ones!"

Then the others would call back, "Baa! Don't care if they are!"

After a while, his mother, who was a sensible Sheep and had seen much of life, said to him: "You must not brag about your tail. It is very rude of you, and very silly too, for you have exactly such a tail as was given to you, and the other Lambs have exactly such tails as were given to them, and when you are older you will know that it did not matter in the least what kind of tail you wore when you were little." She might have told him something else, but she didn't.

The Lamb didn't dare to boast of his tail after this, but when he passed the others, he would look at his mother, and if he thought she wouldn't see, he would wiggle it at them. Of course that was just as bad as talking about it, and the other Lambs knew perfectly well what he meant; still, they pretended not to understand.

One morning, when his mother's back was turned, he was surprised to see that she had only a short and stumpy tail. He had been thinking so much of his own that he had

not noticed hers. "Mother," he cried, "why didn't you have a long tail too?"

"I did have once," she answered with a sheepish smile.

"Did it get broken?" he asked in a faint little voice. He was thinking how dreadful it would be if he should break his.

"Not exactly," said his mother. "I will tell you all about it. All little Lambs have long tails—"

"Not so long as mine, though," said he, interrupting.

"No, not so long as yours," she replied, "but so long that if they were left that way always they would make a great deal of trouble. As the wool grows on them, they would catch burrs and sharp, prickly things, which would pull the wool and sting the skin. The farmer knows this, so when the little Lambs are about as old as you are now, he and his men make their tails shorter."

"Oh!" cried the Lamb, curling his tail in as far between his legs as he could, "do you mean that they will shorten my tail, my beautiful long tail?"

"That is just what I mean," said his mother, "and you should be very glad of it. When that is done, you will be ready to go out into the field with me. A lot of trouble we should have if the men did not look after such things for us; but that is what men are for, they say,—to look after us Sheep."

"But won't they laugh at me when my tail is shorter?" asked her son.

"They would laugh at you if you wore it long. No Lamb who pretends to be anybody would be seen in the pasture with a dangling tail. Only wild Sheep wear them long, poor things!"

Now the little Lamb wished that he had not boasted so much. Now, when the others passed him, he did not put on airs. Now he wondered why they couldn't have short tails in the beginning. He asked his uncle, an old Wether Sheep, why this was and his uncle laughed. "Why, what would you have done all these days if things happened in that way? What would you have had to think about? What could you have talked about?" The little Lamb hung his head and asked no more questions.

"What do you think?" he called to a group of Lambs near by. "I'm going to have one of the men shorten my tail. It is such a bother unless one does have it done, and mine is so very long!"

THE WONDERFUL SHINY EGG

"CUT-CUT-CA-DAH-CUT! Cut-cut-cut-ca-dah-cut!" called the Dorking Hen, as she strutted around the poultry-yard. She held her head very high, and paused every few minutes to look around in her jerky way and see whether the other fowls were listening. Once she even stood on her left foot right in the pathway of the Shanghai Cock, and cackled into his very ears.

Everybody pretended not to hear her. The people in the poultry-yard did not like the Dorking Hen very well. They said that she put on airs. Perhaps she did. She certainly talked a great deal of the place from which she and the Dorking Cock came. They had come in a small cage from a large poultry farm, and the Dorking Hen never tired of telling about the wonderful, noisy ride that they took in a dark car drawn by a great, black, snorting creature. She said that this creature's feet grew on to his sides and whirled around as he ran, and that he breathed out of the top of his head. When the fowls first heard of this, they were much interested, but after a while they used to walk away from her, or make believe that they saw Grasshoppers whom they wanted to chase.

When she found that people were not listening to her, she cackled louder than ever, "Cut-cut-ca-dah-cut! Look at the egg—the egg—the egg—the egg that I have laid."

"Is there any particular reason why we should look at the egg—the egg—the egg—the egg that you have laid?"

asked the Shanghai Cock, who was the grumpiest fowl in the yard.

Now, usually if the Dorking Hen had been spoken to in this way, she would have ruffled up her head feathers and walked away, but this time she had news to tell and so she kept her temper. "Reason?" she cackled. "Yes indeed! It is the finest egg that was ever laid in this poultry-yard."

"Hear her talk!" said a Bantam Hen. "I think it is in very poor taste to lay such large eggs as most of the Hens do here. Small ones are much more genteel."

"She must forget an egg that I laid a while ago with two yolks," said a Shanghai Hen. "That was the largest egg ever laid here, and I have always wished that I had hatched it. A pair of twin chickens would have been so interesting."

"Well," said the Dorking Hen, who could not keep still any longer, "small eggs may be genteel and large ones may be interesting, but my last one is bee-autiful."

"Perhaps you'd just as soon tell us about it as to brag without telling?" grumbled the Shanghai Cock. "I suppose it is grass color, or sky color, or hay color, or speckled, like a sparrow's egg."

"No," answered the Dorking Hen, "it is white, but it is shiny."

"Shiny!" they exclaimed. "Who ever heard of a shiny egg?"

"Nobody," she replied, "and that is why it is so wonderful."

"Don't believe it," said the Shanghai Cock, as he turned away and began scratching the ground.

Now the Dorking Hen did get angry. "Come to see it, if you don't believe me," she said, as she led the others into the Hen-house.

She flew up to the row of boxes where the Hens had their nests, and picked her way along daintily until she reached the farthest one. "Now look," said she.

One by one the fowls peeped into the box, and sure enough, there it lay, a fine, shiny, white egg. The little Bantam, who was really a jolly, kind-hearted creature, said, "Well, it is a beauty. I should be proud of it myself."

"It is whiter than I fancy," said the Shanghai Cock, "but it certainly does shine."

"I shall hatch it," said the Dorking Hen, very decidedly. "I shall hatch it and have a beautiful Chicken with shining feathers. I shall not hatch all the eggs in the nest, but roll this one away and sit on it."

"Perhaps," said one of her friends, "somebody else may have laid it after all, and not noticed. You know it is not the only one in the nest."

"Pooh!" said the Dorking Hen. "I guess I know! I am sure it was not there when I went to the nest and it was there when I left. I must have laid it."

The fowls went away, and she tried to roll the shiny one away from the other eggs, but it was slippery and very light and would not stay where she put it. Then she got out of patience and rolled all the others out of the nest. Two of them fell to the floor and broke, but she did not care. "They are nothing but common ones, anyway," she said.

When the farmer's wife came to gather the eggs she pecked at her and was very cross. Every day she did this, and at last the woman let her alone. Every-day she told the other fowls what a wonderful Chicken she expected to have. "Of course he will be of my color," said she, "but his feathers will shine brightly. He will be a great flyer, too. I am sure that is what it means when the egg is light." She came off the nest each day just long enough to stroll around and chat with her friends, telling them what wonderful things she expected, and never letting them forget that it was she who had laid the shiny egg. She pecked airily at the food, and seemed to think that a Hen who was hatching such a wonderful Chicken should have the best of everything. Each day she told some new beauty that was to belong to her child, until the Shanghai Cock fairly flapped his wings with impatience.

Day after day passed, and the garden beyond the barn showed rows of sturdy green plants, where before there had been only straight ridges of fine brown earth. The Swallows who were building under the eaves of the great barn, twittered and chattered of the wild flowers in the forest, and four other Hens came off their nests with fine broods of downy Chickens. And still the Dorking Hen sat on her shiny egg and told what a wonderful Chicken she expected to hatch. This was not the only egg in the nest now, but it was the only one of which she spoke.

At last a downy Chicken peeped out of one of the common eggs, and wriggled and twisted to free himself from the shell. His mother did not hurry him or help him. She knew that he must not slip out of it until all the blood from the shell-lining had run into his tender little body. If she had pushed the shell off before he had all of this fine red blood, he would not have been a strong Chicken, and she wanted her children to be strong.

The Dorking Cock walked into the Hen-house and stood around on one foot. He came to see if the shiny egg had hatched, but he wouldn't ask. He thought himself too dignified to show any interest in newly hatched Chickens before a Hen. Still, he saw no harm in standing around on one foot and letting the Dorking Hen talk to him if she wanted to. When she told him it was one of the common eggs that had hatched, he was quite disgusted, and stalked out of doors without a word.

The truth was that he had been rather bragging to the other Cocks, and only a few minutes later he spoke with pride of the time when "our" shiny egg should hatch. "For," he said, "Mrs. Dorking and I have been quite alone here as far as our own people are concerned. It is not strange that we should feel a great pride in the wonderful egg and the Chicken to be hatched from it. A Dorking is a Dorking after all, my friends." And he flapped his wings, stretched his neck, and crowed as loudly as he could.

"Yes," said the Black Spanish Cock afterward, "a Dorking certainly is a Dorking, although I never could see the sense of making such a fuss about it. They are fat and they have an extra toe on each foot. Why should a fowl want extra toes? I have four on each foot, and I can scratch up all the food I want with them."

"Well," said the grumpy old Shanghai Cock, "I am sick and tired of this fuss. Common eggs are good enough for Shanghais and Black Spanish and Bantams, and I should think—"

Just at this minute they heard a loud fluttering and squawking in the Hen-house and the Dorking Hen crying, "Weasel! Weasel!" The Cocks ran to drive the Weasel away, and the Hens followed to see it done. All was noise and hurry, and they saw nothing of the Weasel except the tip of his bushy tail as he drew his slender body through an opening in the fence.

The Dorking Hen was on one of the long perches where the fowls roost at night, the newly hatched Chicken lay shivering in the nest, and on the floor were the pieces of the wonderful shiny egg. The Dorking Hen had knocked it from the nest in her flight.

The Dorking Cock looked very cross. He was not afraid of a Weasel, and he did not see why she should be. "Just like a Hen!" he said.

The Black Spanish Hen turned to him before he could say another word. "Just like a Cock!" she exclaimed. "I never raise Chickens myself. It is not the custom among the Black Spanish Hens. We lay the eggs and somebody else hatches them. But if I had been on the nest as long as Mrs. Dorking has, do you suppose I'd let any fowl speak to me as you spoke to her? I'd—I'd—" and she was so angry that she couldn't say another word, but just strutted up and down and cackled.

A motherly old Shanghai Hen flew up beside Mrs. Dorking. "We are very sorry for you," she said. "I know how I should have felt if I had broken my two-yolked egg just as it was ready to hatch."

The Bantam Hen picked her way to the nest. "What a dear little Chicken!" she cried, in her most comforting tone. "He is so plump and so bright for his age. But, my dear, he is chilly, and I think you should cuddle him under your wings until his down is dry."

The Dorking Hen flew down. "He is a dear," she said, "and yet when he was hatched I didn't care much for him, because

I had thought so long about the shiny egg. It serves me right to lose that one, because I have been so foolish. Still, I do not know how I could stand it if it were not for my good neighbors."

While Mrs. Dorking was talking with the Bantam by her nest, the Black Spanish Hen scratched a hole in the earth under the perches, poked the pieces of the shiny egg into it, and covered them up. "I never raise Chickens myself," she said, "but if I did—"

The Shanghai Cock walked away with the Dorking Cock. "I'm sorry for you," he said, "and I am more sorry for Mrs. Dorking. She is too fine a Hen to be spoken to as you spoke to her this morning, and I don't want to hear any more of your fault-finding. Do you understand?" And he ruffled his neck feathers and stuck his face close to that of the Dorking Cock. They stared into each other's eyes for a minute; then the Dorking Cock, who was not so big and strong as the Shanghai, shook his head and answered sweetly, "It was rude of me. I won't do it again."

From that day to this, nobody in the poultry yard has ever spoken of the shiny egg, and the Dorkings are much liked by the other fowls. Yet if it had not been for her trouble, Mrs. Dorking and her neighbors would never have become such good friends. The little Dorkings are fine, fat-breasted Chicks, with the extra toe on each foot of which all that family are so proud.

THE DUCKLING WHO DIDN'T KNOW WHAT TO DO

"Quack! Quack!" called the Duck who had been sitting on her nest so long. "My first egg is cracked, and I can see the broad yellow bill of my eldest child. Ah! Now I can see his downy white head." The Drake heard her and quacked the news to every one around, and flapped his wings, and preened his feathers, for was not this the first Duckling ever hatched on the farm?

The Drake had not been there long himself. It was only a few days before the Duck began sitting that she and her five sisters had come with him to this place. It had not taken them long to become acquainted with the other farmyard people, and all had been kind to them. The Geese had rather put on airs, at first, because they were bigger and had longer legs, but the Ducks and Drake were too wise to notice this in any way, and before long the Geese were as friendly as possible. They would have shown the Ducks the way to the water if it had been necessary, but it was not, for Ducks always know without being told just where to find it. They know, and they do not know why they know. It is one of the things that are.

Now that the first Duckling had chipped the shell, everybody wanted to see him, and there was soon a crowd of fowls around the nest watching him free himself from it.

The Drake stood by, as proud as a Peacock. "I think he looks much like his mother," said he.

"Yes, yes," cackled all the Hens. "The same broad yellow bill, the same short yellow legs, and the same webbed feet."

The mother Duck smiled. "He looks more like me now than he will by and by," she said, "for when his feathers grow and cover the down, he will have a stiff little one curled up on his back like the Drake's. And really, except for the curled feather, his father and I look very much alike."

"That is so," said the Black Spanish Cock. "You do look alike; the same white feathers, the same broad breast, the same strong wings, the same pointed tail, the same long neck, the same sweet expression around the bill!" That was just like the Black Spanish Cock. He always said something pleasant about people when he could, and it was much better than saying unpleasant things. Indeed, he was the most polite fowl in the poultry-yard, and the Black Spanish Hen thought his manners quite perfect.

Then the Duckling's five aunts pushed their way through the crowd to the nest under the edge of the strawstack. "Have you noticed what fine large feet he has?" said one of them. "That is like his mother's people. See what a strong web is between the three long toes on each foot! He will be a good swimmer. The one toe that points backward is small, to be sure, but he does not need that in swimming. That is only to make waddling easier."

"Yes, yes," "A fine web," and "Very large feet," cried the fowls around the nest, but most of them didn't care so much about the size of his feet as the Ducks did. Large feet are always useful, you know, yet nobody needs them so badly as Geese and Ducks. The Geese were off swimming, and so could not see the Duckling when first he came out of the shell.

"Tap-tap, tap-tap," sounded inside another shell, and they knew that there would soon be a second damp little Duckling beside the first. The visitors could not stay to see this one come out, and they went away for a time. The eldest Duckling had supposed that this was life, to have people around saying, "How bright he is!" "What fine legs!" or "He has a beautiful bill!" And now that they all walked away and his mother was looking after the Duckling who was just breaking her shell, he didn't like it—he didn't like it at all.

Still, it was much better so. If he had had no brothers and sisters, he would have been a lonely little fellow; besides, he would have had his own way nearly all the time, and that is likely to make any Duckling selfish. Then, too, if all the other fowls had petted him and given him the best of everything, he would have become vain. Truly, it was a good thing for him not to be the only child, and he soon learned to think so.

After there were two Ducklings, a third one came, and a fourth, and a fifth, and so on until, when the broken shells were cleared away and the mother had counted bills, she could call to the Drake and her sisters, "Nine Ducklings hatched, and there were only nine eggs in the nest."

"Then come to the brook," said the Drake, "and let the children have a bath. I have been swimming a great many times to-day, and they have not even set foot in water yet. Why, our eldest son was out of his shell before the Horses were harnessed this morning, and here it is nearly time for their supper."

"I couldn't help it," said the mother Duck. "I couldn't leave the nest to take him swimming until the rest were ready to go. I am doing the best I can."

"I didn't mean to find fault," said the Drake, "and I suppose you couldn't get away, but we know that Ducklings should be taught to bathe often, and there is nothing like beginning in time."

"I might have taken some of them to the brook," said one of the aunts. The mother straightened her neck and held her head very high, while she answered, "You? You are very kind, but what do you know about bringing up Ducklings?"

Now the aunt might have said, "I know just as much as you do," for it was the young mother's first brood, yet she kept still. She thought, "I may hatch Ducklings of my own some day, and then I suppose I shall want to care for them myself."

"Wait," said the Drake, as they reached the brook. "Let us wait and see what the children will do." The words were hardly out of his bill when—flutter—splash—splash!—there were nine yellow-white Ducklings floating on the brook and murmuring happily to each other as though they had never done anything else.

The Dorking Cock stood on the bank. "Who taught them to swim?" said he.

"Nobody," answered their mother proudly. "They knew without being told. That is the way a Duck takes to water." And she gave a dainty lurch and was among her brood.

"Well!" exclaimed the Dorking Cock. "I thought the

little Dorkings were as bright as children could be, but they didn't know as much as that. I must tell them." He stalked off, talking under his breath.

"They know more than that," said the Drake. "Did you see how they ran ahead of us when we stopped to talk? They knew where to find water as soon as they were out of the shell. Still, the Cock might not have believed that if I had told him."

They had a good swim, and then all stood on the bank and dried themselves. This they did by squeezing the water out of their down with their bills. The Drake, the mother Duck, the five aunts, and the nine Ducklings all stood as tall and straight as they could, and turned and twisted their long necks, and flapped their wings, and squeezed their down, and murmured to each other. And their father didn't tell the little ones how, and their mother didn't tell them how, and their five aunts didn't tell them how, but they knew without being told.

The Ducklings grew fast, and made friends of all the farmyard people. Early every morning they went to the brook. They learned to follow the brook to the river, and here were wonderful things to be seen. There was plenty to eat, too, in the soft mud under the water, and it was easy enough to dive to it, or to reach down their long necks while only their pointed tails and part of their body could be seen above the water. Not that they ate the mud. They kept only the food that they found in it, and then let the mud slip out between the rough edges of their bills. They swam and ate all day, and slept all night, and were dutiful Ducklings who minded their mother, so it was not strange that they were plump and happy.

At last there came a morning when the eldest Duckling could not go to the brook with the others. A Weasel had bitten him in the night, and if it had not been for his mother and the Drake, would have carried him away. The rest had to go in swimming, and his lame leg would not let him waddle as far as the brook, or swim after he got there.

"I don't know what to do," he said to his mother. "I can't swim and I can't waddle far, and I've eaten so much already that I can't eat anything more for a long, long time."

"You might play with the little Shanghais," said his mother.

"They run around too much," he replied. "I can't keep up with them."

"Then why not lie near the corn crib and visit with the Mice?"

"Oh, they don't like the things that I like, and it isn't any fun."

"How would it suit you to watch the Peacock for a while?"

"I'm tired of watching the Peacock."

"Then," said the mother, "you must help somebody else. You are old enough to think of such things now, and you must remember this wise saying: 'When you don't know what to do, help somebody.'"

"Whom can I help?" said the lame Duckling. "People can all do things for themselves."

"There is the Blind Horse," answered his mother. "He is alone to-day, and I'm sure he would like somebody to visit him."

"Quack!" said the Duckling. "I will go to see him." He waddled slowly away, stopping now and then to rest, and shaking his little pointed tail from side to side as Ducks do. The Blind Horse was grazing in the pasture alone.

"I've come to see you, sir," said the Duckling. "Shall I be in your way?"

The Blind Horse looked much pleased. "I think from your voice that you must be one of the young Ducks," said he. "I shall be very glad to have you visit me, only you must be careful to keep away from my feet, for I can't see, and I might step on you."

"I'll be careful," said the Duckling. "I can't waddle much anyway this morning, because my leg hurts me so."

"Why, I'm sorry you are lame," said the Horse. "What is the matter?"

"A Weasel bit me in the night, sir. But it doesn't hurt so much as it did before I came to see you. Perhaps the pasture is a better place for lame legs than the farmyard." He didn't know that it was because he was trying to make somebody else happy that he felt so much better, yet that was the reason.

The Blind Horse and the Duckling became very fond of each other and had a fine time. The Horse told stories of his Colthood, and of the things he had seen in his travels before he became blind. And the Duckling told him what the other farmyard people were doing, and about the soft, fleecy clouds that drifted across the blue sky. When the mother Duck came to look for him, the little fellow was much surprised. "Didn't you go to the brook?" he asked.

"Yes," said his mother, with a smile. "We have been there all the morning. Don't you see how high the sun is?"

"Why-ee!" said the Duckling. "I didn't think I had been here long at all. We've been having the nicest time. And

I'm coming again, am I not?" He asked this question of the Blind Horse.

"I wish you would come often," answered the Blind Horse. "You have given me a very pleasant morning. Good-bye!"

The mother Duck and her son waddled off together. "How is your leg?" said she.

"I forgot all about it until I began to walk," answered the Duckling. "Isn't that queer?"

"Not at all," said his mother. "It was because you were making somebody else happy. 'When you don't know what to do, help somebody.'"

THE FUSSY QUEEN BEE

IN a sheltered corner of the farmyard, where the hedge kept off the cold winds and the trees shaded from hot summer sunshine, there were many hives of Bees. One could not say much for the Drones, but the others were the busiest of all the farmyard people, and they had so much to do that they did not often stop to visit with their neighbors.

In each hive, or home, there were many thousand Bees, and each had his own work. First of all, there was the Queen. You might think that being a Queen meant playing all the time, but that is not so, for to be a really good Queen, even in a Beehive, one must know a great deal and keep at work all the time. The Queen Bee is the mother of all the Bee Babies, and she spends her days in laying eggs. She is so very precious and important a person that the first duty of the rest is to take care of her.

The Drones are the stoutest and finest-looking of all the Bees, but they are lazy, very, very lazy. There are never many of them in a hive, and like most lazy people, they spend much of their time in telling the others how to work. They do not make wax or store honey, and as the Worker Bees do not wish them to eat what has been put away for winter, they do not live very long.

Most of the Bees are Workers. They are smaller than

either the Queen Mother or the Drones, and they gather all the honey, make all the wax, build the comb, and feed the babies. They keep the hive clean, and when the weather is very warm, some of them fan the air with their wings to cool it. They guard the doorway of the hive, too, and turn away the robbers who sometimes come to steal their honey.

In these busy homes, nobody can live long just for himself. Everybody helps somebody else, and that makes life pleasant. The Queen Mother often lays as many as two thousand eggs in a day. Most of these are Worker eggs, and are laid in the small cells of the brood comb, which is the nursery of the hive. A few are Drone eggs and are laid in large cells. She never lays any Queen eggs, for she does not want more Queens growing up. It is a law among the Bees that there can be only one grown Queen living in each home.

The Workers, however, know that something might happen to their old Queen Mother, so, after she has gone away, they sometimes go into a cell where she has laid a Worker egg, and take down the waxen walls between it and the ones on either side to make a very large royal cell. They bite away the wax with their strong jaws and press the rough edges into shape with their feet. When this egg hatches, they do not feed the baby, or Larva, with tasteless bread made of flower-dust, honey, and water, as they would if they intended it to grow up a Worker or a Drone. Instead, they make what is called royal jelly, which is quite sour, and tuck this all around the Larva, who now looks like a little white worm.

The royal jelly makes her grow fast, and in five days she

is so large as to nearly fill the cell. Then she stops eating, spins a cocoon, and lies in it for about two and a half days more. When she comes out of this, she is called a Pupa. Sixteen days after the laying of the egg, the young Queen is ready to come out of her cell. It takes twenty-one days for a Worker to become fully grown and twenty-five for a Drone.

In the hive by the cedar tree, the Queen Mother was growing restless and fussy. She knew that the Workers were raising some young Queens, and she tried to get to the royal cells. She knew that if she could only do that, the young Queens would never live to come out. The Workers knew this, too, and whenever she came near there, they made her go away.

The Queen Larvæ and Pupæ were of different ages, and one of them was now ready to leave her cell. They could hear her crying to be let out, but they knew that if she and the Queen Mother should meet now, one of them would die. So instead of letting her out, they built a thick wall of wax over the door and left only an opening through which they could feed her. When she was hungry she ran her tongue out and they put honey on it.

She wondered why the Workers did not let her out, when she wanted so much to be free. She did not yet know that Queen Mothers do not get along well with young Queens.

The Workers talked it over by themselves. One of them was very tender-hearted. "It does seem too bad," said she, "to keep the poor young Queen shut up in her cell. I don't see how you can stand it to hear her piping so pitifully all the time. I am sure she must be beautiful. I never saw a finer tongue than the one she runs out for honey."

"Humph!" said a sensible old Worker, who had seen

many Queens hatched and many swarms fly away, "you'd be a good deal more sorry if we did let her out now. It would not do at all."

The tender-hearted Worker did not answer this, but she talked it over with the Drones. "I declare," said she, wiping her eyes with her forefeet, "I can hardly gather a mouthful of honey for thinking of her."

"Suppose you hang yourself up and make wax then," said one Drone. "It is a rather sunshiny day, but you ought to be doing something, and if you cannot gather honey you might do that." This was just like a Drone. He never gathered honey or made wax, yet he could not bear to see a Worker lose any time.

The Worker did not hang herself up and make wax, however. She never did that except on cloudy days, and she was one of those Bees who seem to think that nothing will come out right unless they stop working to see about it. There was plenty waiting to be done, but she was too sad and anxious to do it. She might have known that since her friends were only minding the law, it was right to keep the new Queen in her cell.

The Queen Mother was restless and fussy. She could not think of her work, and half the time she did not know whether she was laying a Drone egg or a Worker egg. In spite of that, she did not make any mistake, or put one into the wrong kind of cell. "I cannot stay here with a young Queen," said she. "I will not stay here. I will take my friends with me and fly away."

Whenever she met a Worker, she struck her feelers on those of her friend, and then this friend knew exactly how she felt about it. In this way the news was passed around, and soon many of the Workers were as restless as their Queen Mother. They were so excited over it at times that the air of the hive grew very hot. After a while they would become quiet and gather honey once more. They whispered often to each other. "Do you know where we are going?" one said.

"Sh!" was the answer. "The guides are looking for a good place now."

"I wish the Queen Mother knew where we are going," said the first.

"How could she?" replied the second. "You know very well that she has not left the hive since she began to lay eggs. Here she comes now."

"Oh dear!" exclaimed the Queen Mother. "I can never stand this. I certainly cannot. To think I am not allowed to rule in my own hive! The Workers who are guarding the royal cells drive me away whenever I go near them. I will not stay any longer."

"Then," said a Drone, as though he had thought of it for the first time, "why don't you go away?"

"I shall," said she. "Will you go with me?"

"No," said the Drone. "I hate moving and furnishing a new house. Besides, somebody must stay here to take care of the Workers and the young Queen."

The Queen Mother walked away. "When we were both young," she said to herself, "he would have gone anywhere with me."

And the Drone said to himself, "Now, isn't that just like a Queen Mother! She has known all the time that there would be young Queens coming on, and that she would have to leave, yet here she is, making the biggest kind of fuss about it. She ought to remember that it is the law."

Indeed she should have remembered that it was the law, for everything is done by law in the hive, and no one person should find fault. The law looks after them all, and will not let any one have more than his rightful share.

That same afternoon there was a sudden quiet in their home. The Workers who had been outside returned and visited with the rest. While they were waiting, a few who were to be their guides came to the door of the hive, struck their wings together, and gave the signal for starting. Then all who were going with the Queen Mother hurried out of the door and flew with her in circles overhead. "Good-bye!" they called. "Raise all the young Queens you wish. We shall never come back. We are going far, far away, and we shall not tell you where. It is a lovely place, a very lovely place."

"Let them go," said the Drones who stayed behind. "Now, isn't it time to let out the young Queen?"

"Not yet," answered a Worker, who stood near the door. "Not one feeler shall she put outside her cell until that swarm is out of sight."

The tender-hearted Worker came up wiping her eyes. "Oh, that poor Queen Mother!" said she. "I am so sorry for her. I positively cannot gather honey to-day, I feel so badly about her going."

"Better keep on working," said her friend. "It's the best thing in the world for that sad feeling. Besides, you should try to keep strong."

"Oh, I will try to eat something from the comb," was the answer, "but I don't feel like working."

"Zzzt!" said the other Worker. "I think if you can eat, you can hunt your food outside, and not take honey we have laid up for winter or food that will be needed for the children."

The Drones chuckled. It was all right for them to be lazy, they thought, but they never could bear to see a Worker waste time. "Ah," cried one of them suddenly, "what is the new swarm doing now?"

The words were hardly out of his mouth when the Queen Mother crawled into the hive again. "Such dreadful luck!" said she. "A cloud passed over the sun just as we were alighting on a tree to rest."

"I wouldn't have come back for that," said a Drone.

"No," said she, in her airiest way, "I dare say you wouldn't, but I would. I dare not go to a new home after a cloud has passed over the sun. I think it is a sign of bad luck. I should never expect a single egg to hatch if I went on. We shall try it again to-morrow."

All the others came back with her, and the hive was once more crowded and hot. "Oh dear!" said the tender-hearted Worker, "isn't it too bad to think they couldn't go?"

The next morning they started again and were quite as excited over it as before. The Queen Mother had fussed and fidgeted all the time, although she had laid nine hundred and seventy-three eggs while waiting, and that in spite of interruptions. "Being busy keeps me from thinking," said she, "and I must do something." This time the Queen Mother lighted on an apple-tree branch, and the others clung to her until all who had left the hive were in a great mass on the branch,—a mass as large as a small cabbage. They meant to rest a little while and then fly away to the new home chosen by their guides.

While they were hanging here, the farmer came under the tree, carrying a long pole with a wire basket fastened to the upper end. He shook the clustered Bees gently into it, and then changed them into an empty hive that stood beside their old home.

"Now," said the Workers who had stayed in the old hive, "we will let out the new Queen, for the Queen Mother will never return."

It did not take long to bite away the waxen wall and let her out. Then they gathered around and caressed her, and touched their feelers to her and waited upon her, and explained why they could not let her out sooner. She was still a soft gray color, like all young Bees when they first come from the cell, but this soon changed to the black worn by her people.

The Workers flew in and out, and brought news from the hive next door. They could not go there, for the law does not allow a Bee who lives in one home to visit in another, but they met their old friends in the air or when they were sipping honey. They found that the Queen Mother had quite given up the idea of living elsewhere and was as busy as ever. The farmer had put a piece of comb into the new hive so that she could begin housekeeping at once.

The new Queen was petted and kept at home until she was strong and used to moving about. That was not long. Then she said she wanted to see the world outside. "We will go with you," said the Drones, who were always glad of an excuse for flying away in pleasant weather. They said there was so much noise and hurrying around in the hive that they could never get any real rest there during the daytime.

So the young Queen flew far away and saw the beautiful world for the first time. Such a blue sky! Such green grass! Such fine trees covered with sweet-smelling blossoms! She loved it all as soon as she saw it. "Ah," she cried, "what a wonderful thing it is to live and see all this! I am so glad that I was hatched. But now I must hurry home, for there is so much to be done."

She was a fine young Queen, and the Bees were all proud of her. They let her do anything she wished as long as she kept away from the royal cells. She soon began to work as the old Queen Mother had done, and was very happy in her own way. She would have liked to open the royal cells and prevent more Queens from hatching, and when they told her it was the law which made them keep her away, she still wanted to bite into them.

"That poor young Queen Mother!" sighed the tender-hearted Worker. "I am so sorry for her when she is kept away from the royal cells. This is a sad, sad world!" But this isn't a sad world by any means. It is a beautiful, sunshiny, happy world, and neither Queen Bees nor anybody else should think it hard if they cannot do every single thing they wish. The law looks after great and small, and there is no use in pouting because we cannot do one certain thing, when there is any amount of delightful work and play awaiting us. And the young Queen Mother knew this.

THE BAY COLT LEARNS TO MIND

THE span of Bays were talking together in their stalls, and the other Horses were listening. That was one trouble with living in the barn, you could not say anything to your next-door neighbor without somebody else hearing. The farmer had solid walls between the stalls, with openings so far back that no Horse could get his head to them without breaking his halter. This had been done to keep them from biting each other, and as nobody but the Dappled Gray ever thought of doing such a thing, it was rather hard on the rest. It made it difficult for the mothers to bring up their children properly, for after a Colt was old enough to have a stall to himself, his mother had to call out her advice and warnings so loudly that everybody could hear, and you know it is not well to reprove a child before company if it can be helped. Indeed, it was this very question that was troubling the span of Bays now. Each of them had a two-year-old Colt, and they knew that it was nearly time for the farmer to put these Colts to work. The span of Bays were sisters, so of course their children were cousins, and they were all very fond of each other and of the Blind Horse, who was the uncle of the Bays and the great-uncle of the Bay Colt and the Gray Colt.

"I am worried about the Bay Colt," said his mother. "Since he was brought into the barn last fall and had a stall away from me, he has gotten into bad ways. I have told him again and again that he must not nibble the edge of the manger, yet the first thing I heard this morning was the grating of his teeth on the wood."

"Well," said his aunt, "you know he is teething, and that may be the reason."

"That is no excuse," said his mother sternly. "He has been teething ever since he was five days old, and he will not cut his last tooth for three years yet. I don't call it goodness to keep from cribbing when you don't want to crib, and the time to stop is now. Besides, if he waits until he has all his teeth, he won't be able to break himself of the habit when he does try."

"That is so," said his aunt, "and he will ruin his teeth, too."

"Pooh!" exclaimed the Bay Colt, who had heard what they were saying. "I can stop whenever I want to, and they're my own teeth, anyway. It isn't anybody else's business if I do ruin them."

"There!" said his mother to his aunt, "you see what I mean. That is just the way he talks all the time. Now what would you do?"

"Let him alone," snorted the Dappled Gray. "Let him alone, and he will get some Horse sense after he has been broken. He'll have a hard time of it, but he'll come out all right."

The Bay Colt kicked against the side of the stall, he was so vexed. "I'll thank you to let me alone," said he. "I don't see why everybody tells me what I ought to do. Guess I know a thing or two."

"I'll tell you why," said the Dappled Gray, in a voice that sounded as though he were trying very hard not to lose his temper. "It is because you are young and we like you, and we can save you trouble if you mind what we tell you. I had lost the black pits in my front teeth before you were born, and when a Horse has lived long enough to lose the black pits from his front teeth, he knows a good deal. You don't know a curb-bit from a snaffle now, but you will learn many things when you are broken—a very great many things."

The Bay Colt tossed his head and did not answer. When he was led out to drink, the Dappled Gray spoke quickly to his friends. "We will let him alone," said he, "as he wishes. We will not advise him until he asks us to do so." They were all whinnying "Yes" when the Bay Colt came back. Then it became so still that you could have heard a stem of hay drop.

For a few days after this, the Bay Colt had a very good time. Nobody gave him any advice, and even when he gnawed at the edge of the manger, his mother did not seem to notice it. After he found that she didn't say anything, he didn't gnaw, or crib, so much. He was such a foolish and contrary young fellow that when people told him not to do a thing, he always wanted to do that thing worse than anything else in the world. His cousin, the Gray Colt, was not at all like him. She was a gentle little two-year-old whom everybody loved. She was full of fun and was the gayest possible companion in the meadow, yet when the older Horses gave her advice, she always listened and obeyed.

The Bay Colt was very fond of his cousin, but he did like to tease her, and once in the fall, before they came to stay in the barn, he called her a "goody-goody" because she wouldn't jump the fence and run away with him. He said she wouldn't do such things because she didn't know what fun was. Then she did show that she had a temper, for her brown eyes snapped and her soft lips were raised until she showed all her biting teeth. "I'm not a 'goody-goody,'" she cried, stamping the ground with her pretty little hoofs, "and I just ache to go. I feel as though there were ropes that I couldn't see, pulling me toward that fence every time I think of it, but I won't go! I won't go! My mother says that she jumped a fence and ran away when she was a Colt, and that she felt as mean as could be afterward."

"I don't care," said her cousin, "I'm going anyway, and you can stay at home if you want to. Good-bye!" He ran and leaped over the fence, and trotted down the road with his head well up and his tail in the air. And then how the Gray Colt did want to follow! "I won't!" she said again. "I won't do it. I'll look the other way and try to forget it, but I wish he knew how hard it is to be good sometimes."

The next morning the Bay Colt was in the pasture again. The farmer and his man had found him far away and led him back. "I had a fine time," he said to his cousin, "and I don't feel a bit mean. I'm going again to-day, but don't you tell." When his mother scolded him as he deserved, he just switched his tail and thought about something else until she stopped talking. Then he ran away again.

The next morning when the Gray Colt saw him, he had a queer wooden thing around his neck, and fastened to this was a pole that stuck out ahead of him. It tired his neck and bothered him when he wanted to run. If he had tried to jump the fence, it would have thrown him down. When the Gray Colt came toward him, he pretended not to see her. He might just as well have looked squarely at her as soon as she came, because, you know, he had to look at her sometime, but he had a mean, slinking, afraid feeling, such as people always have when they have done something wrong and have had time to think about it. Besides, he had changed his mind since the wooden poke had been put on him, and somehow his running away seemed very foolish now. He wondered how he could ever have thought it any fun, and he was so disgusted that he couldn't keep his ears still, but moved them restlessly when he remembered his own silliness.

The Gray Colt was too polite to say anything about his wearing the poke, and she talked about the grass, the sky, the trees, and everything else she could think of. Once she was about to speak of the fence, and then she remembered and stopped short. The Bay Colt noticed this. "You might just as well go on," said he. "You are very kind, but I know how foolish I have been, and there's no use in keeping still. You were right, and it doesn't pay to jump fences for a few minutes of what you think will be fun. I feel sick all over when I think about it."

"It's too bad," whinnied the Gray Colt. "I'm very sorry for you."

"And what do you think?" said the Bay Colt. "I heard the Dappled Gray say this morning that I was like a Pig! Imagine a Colt being like a Pig! He said that it didn't make any difference on which side of a fence Pigs were, they always wanted to be on the other side, and that I was just as stupid."

This was all in the fall, before the cold weather had sent them to live in the barn, and while the Bay Colt was wearing the poke he could not well forget the lesson he had learned about jumping and running away. His mother grew quite proud of him, and the Dappled Gray had been heard to say that he might amount to something yet. That was a great deal for the Dappled Gray to say, for although he had a very kind heart, he did not often praise people, and hardly ever said such things about two-year-olds. That made it all the harder for him when the Bay Colt became cross over being told to stop cribbing.

You know there are some Colts who learn obedience easily, and there are others who have one hard struggle to stop jumping, and another to stop cribbing, and another to stop kicking, and so on, all through their Colthood. The older Horses are sorry for them and try to help them, for they know that neither Colt nor Horse can really enjoy life until he is trying to do right. To be sure, people sometimes do wrong even then, but if they will take advice and keep on trying they are certain to turn out well.

And now, when the Bay Colt seemed to have forgotten the lesson he had in the fall, and after he had told the other Horses to let him alone, very strange things began to happen. The farmer took him from his stall and made him open his mouth. Then a piece of iron was slipped into it, which lay on top of his tongue and fitted into the place on each side of his jaw where there were no teeth. Long lines were fastened to this iron on either side, and when he tossed his head and sidled around, these lines were gently pulled by the farmer and the iron bit pressed down his tongue.

The farmer was very kind, but the Bay Colt did not want the bit in his mouth, so he acted as ugly as he knew how, and kicked, and snapped with his jaws open, and tried to run. The farmer did not grow angry or cross, yet whenever the Bay Colt showed his temper, the bit would press down his tongue and stretch the corners of his mouth until he had to stop. Once in a while the farmer would try to pat him and show him that it was all right, but the Bay Colt would not have this, and he was a very cross and sweaty two-year-old when he was taken back to his stall.

He missed the Gray Colt from her usual place, but soon she came in with one of the farmer's men. She had been driven for the first time also.

"Hallo!" said he. "Have you had a bit in your mouth too? Wasn't it dreadful? I am so angry that my hoofs fairly tingle to hit that farmer."

"It was hard," said the Gray Colt, "but the man who drove me was very kind and let me rest often. He patted me, too, and that helped me to be brave. My mother says we won't mind the bit at all after we are used to it."

"Well," said the Bay Colt, "I'm never going to be used to it. I won't stand it, and that's all there is about it." He stamped his hoofs and looked very important. Two-year-olds often look quite as important as ten-year-olds, and they feel much more so. The Bay Colt was rather proud of his feet, and thought it much nicer to have solid hoofs than to have them split, like those of the Cows, the Hogs, and the Sheep.

When he said that he would not stand it to be driven, a queer little sound ran through the stalls. It was like the wind passing over a wheatfield, and was caused by the older Horses taking a long breath and whispering to themselves.

The Bay Colt's mother was saying, "Poor child! What hard work he does make of life!"

The next day both Colts were driven again, and the next day, and the next, and the next. By this time the Gray Colt was quite used to it. She said she rather enjoyed knowing what the man was thinking, and that she could tell his thoughts by the feeling of the lines, much as she used to understand her mother by rubbing noses when she was a tiny Colt. Her cousin had a sore mouth from jerking on the lines, and he could not enjoy eating at all. That made it even harder for him, because he got very hungry, and it is not so easy to be sensible when one is hungry.

When the Gray Colt learned to walk steadily and turn as her driver wished, she was allowed to draw a light log through the furrows of a field. This tired her, but it made her very proud, and she arched her neck and took the daintiest of steps. It was not necessary that the log should be drawn over the field; still, she did not know this, and thought it was real work, when it was done only to teach her to pull. The man who was driving her patted her neck and held her nose in his hand. When he stopped to eat an apple, he gave her the core, and she thought she had never tasted anything so good. As she went back to her stall, she called to the Horses near, "I have been working. I have drawn a log all around a field."

The Blind Horse spoke softly to her. "You will have a happy life, my dear, because you are a willing worker."

Although the Bay Colt didn't say anything, he thought a great deal, and about many things. While he was thinking he began to crib, but the noise of his biting teeth on the wood startled him, and he shook his head and whispered to himself, "I will never crib again." When he ate his supper, his sore mouth hurt him, but he didn't whimper. "You deserve it," he said to himself. "It wouldn't have been sore if you had been steady like your cousin." The Bay Colt was growing sensible very fast.

The Dappled Gray had noticed how suddenly he stopped cribbing, and so watched him for a few days. He saw that the Bay Colt was in earnest, that he drew the log up and down without making any fuss, and was soon hitched with his mother to a plow. The Dappled Gray and the Blind Horse were also plowing that day, and they called across from their field. "Fine day for plowing," they said.

"Perfect," answered the Bay Colt. "Did you notice the last furrow we turned? Can you do any better than that? If I had jumped, it would have been crooked instead of straight; and if I had stopped, it would not be done yet."

"Good furrow! Wonderful furrow!" answered the Dappled Gray. "Always knew you'd be a good worker when you got down to it. You are one of us now, one of the working Horses. Glad of it. Good-bye!" And he turned away to start his plow across the field again.

"Do you like being grown up?" said the Bay Colt's mother to him.

"Like it?" he answered with a laugh. "I'm so proud that I don't know what to do. I wouldn't go back to the old life of all play for anything in the world. And my little cousin made me see my mistakes. Was there ever another Colt as foolish as I?"

"A great many of them," said his mother. "More than you would guess. They kick and bite and try to run because they cannot always have their own way; and then, when they have tried the farmer's way, and begin to pay for his care of them, they find it very much better than the life of all play. Colts will be Colts."

THE TWIN LAMBS

THERE was a Lamb, a bright, frisky young fellow, who had a twin sister. Their mother loved them both and was as kind to one as to the other, but the brother wanted to have the best of everything, and sometimes he even bunted his sister with his hard little forehead. His mother had to speak to him many times about this, for he was one of those trying children who will not mind when first spoken to.

He did not really mean to be naughty—he was only strong and frisky and thoughtless. Sometimes he was even rude to his mother. She felt very sad when this was so, yet she loved him dearly and found many excuses for him in her own heart.

There were three other pairs of twins in the flock that year, and as their mothers were not strong enough to care for two Lambs apiece, the farmer had taken one twin from each pair to a little pen near the house. Here they stayed, playing happily together, and drinking milk from a bottle which the farmer's wife brought to them. They were hungry very often, like all young children, and when their stomachs began to feel empty, or even to feel as if they might feel empty, they crowded against the side of the pen, pushed their pinkish-white noses through the openings between the boards, and bleated and bleated and bleated to the farmer's wife.

Soon she would come from the kitchen door and in her hand would bring the big bottle full of milk for them. There was a soft rubber top to this bottle, through which the Lambs could draw the milk into their mouths. Of course they all wanted to drink at once, though there was only a chance for one, and the others always became impatient while they were waiting. The farmer's wife was patient, even when the Lambs, in their hurry to get the milk, took her fingers into their mouths and bit them instead of the top of the bottle.

Our twin Lamb wanted to have his sister taken into the pen with the other three, and he spoke about it to his mother. "I know how you can manage," said he. "Whenever she comes near you, just walk away from her, and then the farmer will take her up to the pen."

"You selfish fellow!" answered his mother. "Do you want your dear little twin sister to leave us?"

He hung his head for a minute, but replied, "She'd have just as good a time. They have all they can eat up there, and they have lots of fun."

"If you think it is so pleasant in the pen," said his mother, "suppose I begin to walk away from you, and let the farmer take you away. I think your sister would rather stay with me."

"Oh, no!" cried her son. "I don't want to leave my own dear woolly mother! I want to cuddle up to you every night and have you tell me stories about the stars."

"Do you think you love me very much?" said she. "You don't know how to really love yet, for you are selfish, and there is not room in a selfish heart for the best kind of love."

That made the Lamb feel very badly. "I do love her

dearly," he cried, as he stood alone. "I believe I love her ever so much more than my sister does."

That was where the little fellow was mistaken, for although his sister did not talk so much about it, she showed her love in many other ways. If she had been taken from her mother for even a few days, they could never again have had such sweet and happy days together. Sheep look much alike, and they cannot remember each other's faces very long. If a Lamb is taken away from his mother for even a short time, they do not know each other when they meet afterward. Perhaps this is one reason why they keep together so much, for it would be sad indeed not to know one's mother or one's child.

His sister never knew that he had wanted her taken away. She thought he acted queerly sometimes, but she was so loving and unselfish herself that she did not dream of his selfishness. Instead of putting the idea out of his woolly little head, as he could have done by thinking more of other things, the brother let himself think of it more and more. That made him impatient with even his mother, and he often answered her quite crossly. Sometimes, when she spoke to him, he did not answer at all, and that was just as bad.

His mother would sigh and say to herself, "My child is not a comfort to me after all, yet when I looked for the first time into his dear little face, I thought that as long as I had him beside me I should always be happy."

One night, when the weather was fair and warm, the farmer drove all the Sheep and Lambs into the Sheepshed. They had been lying out under the beautiful blue sky at night, and they did not like this nearly so well. They did not understand it either, so they were frightened and bewildered, and bleated often to each other, "What is this for? What is this for?"

The Lambs did not mind it so much, for they were not warmly dressed, but the Sheep, whose wool had been growing for a year and was long and heavy, found it very close and uncomfortable. They did not know that the farmer had a reason for keeping them dry that night while the heavy dew was falling outside. The same thing was done every year, but they could not remember so long as that, and having a poor memory is always hard.

"Stay close to me, children," said the mother of the twins. "I may forget how you look if you are away long."

"It seems to me," said the brother, "that we always have to stay close to you. I never have a bit of fun!"

When they had cuddled down for the night, the twin Lambs slept soundly. Their mother lay awake for a long, long time in the dark, and she was not happy. A few careless words from a selfish little Lamb had made her heart ache. They were not true words either, for during the daytime her children ran with their playmates and had fine frolics. Still, we know that when people are out of patience they often say things that are not really so.

In the morning, men came into the barn, which opened off the Sheep-shed. They had on coarse, old clothing, and carried queer-looking shears in their hands. The Sheep could see them now and then when the door was open. Once the farmer stood in the doorway and seemed to be counting them. This made them huddle together more closely than ever. They could see the men carrying clean yellow straw into the barn and spreading it on the floor. On top of this was stretched a great sheet of clean cloth.

Then the men began to come into the shed and catch the Sheep and carry them into the barn. They were frightened and bleated a good deal, but when one was caught and carried away, although he might struggle hard to free himself, he did not open his mouth. The old Wether Sheep was the first to be taken, and then the young ones who had been Lambs the year before. For a long time not one of the mothers was chosen. Still, nobody knew what would happen next, and so, the fewer Sheep there were left, the more closely they huddled together.

At last, when the young Sheep had all been taken, one of the men caught the mother of the twins and carried her away. She turned her face toward her children, but the door swung shut after her, and they were left with the other Lambs and their mothers. From the barn came the sound of snip-snip-snipping and the murmur of men's voices. Once the twins thought they saw their mother lying on the floor and a man kneeling beside her, holding her head and forelegs under his arm, yet they were not sure of this.

The brother ran to the corner of the shed and put his head against the boards. He suddenly felt very young and helpless. "My dear woolly mother!" he said to himself, over and over, and he wondered if he would ever see her again. He remembered what he had said to her the night before. It seemed to him that he could even now hear his own voice saying crossly, "Seems to me we always have to stay close to you. I never have a bit of fun!" He wished he had not said it. He knew she was a dear mother, and he would have given anything in the world for a chance to stay close to her again.

His sister felt as lonely and frightened as he, but she did not act in the same way. She stood close to a younger Lamb whose mother had just been taken away, and tried to comfort her. One by one the mothers were taken until only the Lambs remained. They were very hungry now, and bleated pitifully. Still the twin brother stood with his head in the corner. He had closed his eyes, but now he opened them, and through a crack in the wall of the shed, he saw some very slender and white-looking Sheep turned into the meadow. At first they acted dizzy, and staggered instead of walking straight; then they stopped staggering and began to frisk. "Can it be?" said he. "It surely is!" For, although he had never in his short life seen a newly shorn Sheep, he began to understand what had happened.

He knew that the men had only been clipping the long wool from the Sheep, and that they were now ready for warm weather. No wonder they frisked when their heavy burdens of wool were carefully taken off.

Now the farmer opened the door into the barn again, and let the Lambs walk through it to the gate of the meadow. They had never before been inside this barn, and the twin brother looked quickly around as he scampered across the floor. He saw some great ragged bundles of wool, and a man was just rolling up the last fleece. He wondered if that had been taken from his mother and was the very one against which he had cuddled when he was cold or frightened.

When they first reached the pasture, the Lambs could not tell which were their mothers. Shearing off their long and dingy fleeces had made such a difference in their looks! The twin brother knew his mother by her way of walking and by her voice, but he could see that his sister did not know her at all. He saw his mother wandering around as though she did not know where to find her children, and a naughty plan came into his head. If he could keep his sister from finding their mother for even a short time, he knew that the farmer would take her up to the pen. He thought he knew just how to do it, and he started to run to her. Then he stopped and remembered how sad and lonely he had been without his mother only a little while before, and he began to pity the Lambs in the pen.

Now his selfishness and his goodness were fighting hard in him. One said, "Send your sister away," and the other, "Take her to your mother." At last he ran as fast as he could toward his sister. "I am good now," he said to himself, "but it may not last long. I will tell her before I am naughty again."

"Oh sister!" cried he. "Come with me to our mother. She doesn't know where to find us."

He saw a happy look on his sister's sad little face, and he was glad that he had done the right thing. They skipped away together, kicking up their heels as they went, and it seemed to the brother that he had never been so happy in his life. He was soon to be happier, though, for when they reached his "new, white mother," as he called her, and his sister told her how he had shown her the way, his mother said, "Now you are a comfort to me. You will be a happier Lamb, too, for you know that a mother's heart is large enough for all her children, and that the more one loves, the better he loves."

"Why, of course," said the twin sister. "What do you mean?"

But the mother never told her, and the brother never told her, and it is hoped that you will keep the secret.

THE VERY SHORT STORY OF THE FOOLISH LITTLE MOUSE

The Mice who lived in the barn and around the granaries had many cousins living on the farm who were pleasant people to know. Any one could tell by looking at them that they were related, yet there were differences in size, in the coloring of their fur, in their voices, and most of all in their ways of living. Some of these cousins would come to visit at the barn in winter, when there was little to eat in the fields. The Meadow Mice never did this. They were friendly with the people who came from the farmyard to graze in the meadow, yet when they were asked to return the call, they said, "No, thank you. We are an out-of-door family, and we never enter houses. We do not often go to the farmyard, but we are always glad to see you here. Come again."

When the Cows are in the meadow, they watch for these tiny people, and stop short if they hear their voices from the grass near by. Of course the Horses are careful, for Horses will never step on any person, large or small, if they can help it. They are very particular about this.

All through the meadow you can see, if you look sharply, shallow winding paths among the grasses, and these paths are worn by the running to and fro of the Meadow Mice. Their homes are in stumps of trees or in the higher ground near the ditches. In these homes the baby Meadow Mice stay until they are large enough to go out into the great world and eat roots, grasses, and seeds with their fathers and mothers. Sometimes they do go out a little way with their mother before this, and they go in a very funny fashion. Of course, when they are babies, they drink warm milk from her body as the children of most four-legged people do. Sometimes a young Meadow Mouse does not want to stop drinking his milk when it is time for his mother to leave the nest, so he just hangs on to her with his tiny, toothless mouth, and when she goes she drags him along on the ground beside her. The ground is rather rough for such soft little babies, and they do not go far in this way, but are glad enough to snuggle down again with their brothers and sisters.

There is no danger of their being lonely, even when their mother is away, for the Meadow Mice have large families, and where there are ten babies of the same age, or even only six, which is thought a small family among their people, it is not possible for one to feel alone.

There were two fine Meadow Mice who built their nest in the bank of a ditch and were much liked by all their relatives. They had raised many children to full-grown Mousehood, and were kind and wise parents. When their children were married and had homes of their own, they still liked to come back to visit. The father and mother were gentle and kindly, as all Mice are, and were almost as handsome as when they first began to gnaw. Nobody could say that he ever saw a bit of dust on either of them.

The brown fur of the upper part of their bodies and the grayish-white fur underneath always lay sleek and tidy, and from their long whiskers to the tips of their hairless tails, they were as dainty as possible. That was one reason why they were so fine-looking, for you know it makes no difference how beautiful one may be in the first place, if he does not try to keep clean he is not pleasant to look at, while many quite plain people are charming because they look well and happy and clean.

Now this pair of Mice had eight Mouse babies in their nest. The babies were no larger than Bumble Bees at first and very pink. This was not because their fur was pink, but only because it was so very short that through it and their thin skin one saw the glow of the red blood in their veins.

"Did you ever see such beautiful babies?" said their mother proudly to her neighbors. "They are certainly the finest I ever had." Her friends smiled, for she always said the same thing whenever she had little ones. Yet they understood, for they had children of their own, and knew that although mothers love all alike, there is always a time when the youngest seems the most promising. That is before they are old enough to be naughty.

The days passed, and the eight baby Meadow Mice ate and slept and pushed each other around, and talked in their sweet, squeaky little voices. They were less pink every day and more the color of their father and mother. They grew, too, so fast that the nest was hardly large enough for them, and the teeth were showing in their tiny pink mouths. Their mother saw that they would soon be ready to go out into the world, and she began to teach them the things they needed to know. She took them outside the nest each pleasant day and gave them lessons in running and gnawing, and showed them how to crouch down on the brown earth and lie still until danger was past. After she had told them many things, she would ask them short questions to make sure that they remembered.

"How many great dangers are there?" she said.

"Five," answered the little Mice.

"What are they?"

"Hawks, Owls, Weasels, Cats, and men."

"Tell me about Hawks."

"Hawks are big birds who seem to float in the air. They have very sharp eyes, and when they see a Mouse they drop suddenly down and catch him. They fly in the daytime."

"Tell me about Owls."

"They are big birds who fly by night without making any noise. They can see from far away, and they catch Mice."

"Tell me about Weasels."

"They are slender little animals, nearly twice as long as a Mouse. They have small heads, four short legs, and sharp claws; have brown fur on their backs and white underneath, and sometimes, when the weather is very cold, they turn white all over."

"Tell me about Cats."

"Cats are very much bigger than Weasels, and are of many colors. They have long tails and whiskers, and dreadful great eyes. They walk on four legs, but make no noise because they have cushions on their feet."

"Tell me about men."

"Men are very big, two-legged people, and when they are fully grown are taller than Cows. They make noise in walking, and they can neither smell nor see us from afar."

"And what are you to do when you see these dangers coming?"

"We are to run away as fast as we can from Hawks, Weasels, Owls, and Cats. If a man comes near us, we are to lie perfectly still and watch him, and are not to move unless we are sure that he sees us or is likely to step on us. Men do not know so much about Mice as the other dangers do."

"And what if you are not sure that some creature is a Hawk, an Owl, a Weasel, or a Cat?"

"If we even think it may be, we are to run."

"When are you to run?"

"At once."

"Say that again."

"We are to run at once."

"Very good. That is all for to-day."

You can see how well the Meadow Mouse mother brought up her children, and how carefully she taught them about life. If they had been wise and always minded her, they would have saved themselves much trouble.

Seven of them were dutiful and obedient, but the largest of the eight, and the finest-looking, liked to decide things for himself, and often laughed at his brothers and sisters for being afraid. Because he was so big and handsome, and spoke in such a dashing way, they sometimes wondered if he didn't know as much as their mother.

One sunshiny day, when all the eight children were playing and feeding together in the short grass, one of them saw a great black bird in the air. "Oh, look!" she cried. "That may be a Hawk. We'd better run."

"Pooh!" said the biggest little Meadow Mouse. "Who's afraid?"

"Mother said to run," they squeaked, and seven long bare tails whisked out of sight under a stump.

"Ho-ho!" said the biggest little Meadow Mouse. "Before I'd be so scared! I dare you to come back! I dare you to—"

Just then the Hawk swooped down. And that is the end of the story, for after that, there was no foolish little Meadow Mouse to tell about.

THE LONELY LITTLE PIG

ONE day the Brown Hog called to her twelve young Pigs and their ten older brothers and sisters, "Look! look! What is in that cage?"

The twenty-two stubby snouts that were thrust through the opening of the rail-fence were quivering with eagerness and impatience. Their owners wished to know all that was happening, and the old mother's eyes were not so sharp as they had once been, so if the Pigs wanted to know the news, they must stop their rooting to find it out. Bits of the soft brown earth clung to their snouts and trembled as they breathed.

"It looks like a Pig," they said, "only it is white."

"It is a Pig then," grunted their mother, as she lay in the shade of an oak tree. "There are white Pigs, although I never fancied the color. It looks too cold and clean. Brown is more to my taste, brown or black. Your poor father was brown and black, and a finer looking Hog I never saw. Ugh! Ugh!" And she buried her eyes in the loose earth. The Pigs looked at her and then at each other. They did not often speak of their father. Indeed the younger ones did not remember him at all. One of the Cows said he had such a bad temper that the farmer sent him away, and it is certain that none of them had seen him since the day he was driven down the lane.

While they were thinking of this and feeling rather sad, the wagon turned into their lane and they could plainly see the Pig inside. She was white and quite beautiful in her piggish way. Her ears stood up stiffly, her snout was as stubby as though it had been broken off, her eyes were very small, and her tail had the right curl. When she squealed they could see her sharp teeth, and when she put her feet up on the wooden bars of her rough cage, they noticed the fine hoofs on the two big toes of each foot and the two little toes high on the back of her legs, each with its tiny hoof. She was riding in great style, and it is no wonder that the twenty-two Brown Pigs with black spots and black feet opened their eyes very wide. They did not know that the farmer brought her in this way because he was in a hurry, and Pigs will not make haste when farmers want them to. The Hogs are a queer family, and the Off Ox spoke truly when he said that the only way to make one hurry ahead is to tie a rope to his leg and pull back, they are so sure to be contrary.

"She's coming here!" the Brown Pigs cried. "Oh, Mother, she's coming here! We're going to see the men take her out of her cage."

The old Hog grunted and staggered to her feet to go with them, but she was fat and slow of motion, so that by the time she was fairly standing, they were far down the field and running helter-skelter by the side of the fence. As she stared dully after them she could see the twenty-two curly tails bobbing along, and she heard the soft patter of eighty-eight sharp little double hoofs on the earth.

"Ugh!" she grunted. "Ugh! Ugh! I am too late to go. Never

mind! They will tell me all about it, and I can take a nap. I haven't slept half the time to-day, and I need rest."

Just as the Mother Hog lay down again, the men lifted the White Pig from the wagon, cage and all, so she began to squeal, and she squealed and squealed and squealed and squealed until she was set free in the field with the Brown Pigs. Nobody had touched her and nobody had hurt her, but it was all so strange and new that she thought it would make her feel better to squeal. When she was out of her cage and in the field, she planted her hoofs firmly in the ground, looked squarely at the Brown Pigs, and grunted a pleasant, good-natured grunt. The Brown Pigs planted their hoofs in the ground and grunted and stared. They didn't ask her to go rooting with them, and not one of the ten big Pigs or the twelve little Pigs said, "We are glad to see you."

There is no telling how long they would have stood there if the Horses had not turned the wagon just then. The minute the wheels began to grate on the side of the box, every Brown Pig whirled around and ran off.

The poor little White Pig did not know what to make of it. She knew that she had not done anything wrong. She wondered if they didn't mean to speak to her.

At first she thought she would run after them and ask to root with them, but then she remembered something her mother had told her when she was so young that she was pink. It was this: "When you don't know what to do, go to sleep." So she lay down and took a nap.

The Brown Pigs did not awaken their mother, and when they stopped in the fence-corner one of them said to their big sister, "What made you run?"

"Oh, nothing," said she.

"And why did you run?" the little Pigs asked their big brother.

"Because," he answered.

After a while somebody said, "Let's go back to where the White Pig is."

"Oh, no," said somebody else, "don't let's! She can come over here if she wants to, and it isn't nearly so nice there."

You see, they were very rude Pigs and not at all well brought up. Their mother should have taught them to think of others and be kind, which is really all there is to politeness. But then, she had very little time left from sleeping, and it took her all of that for eating, so her children had no manners at all.

At last the White Pig opened her round eyes and saw all the Brown Pigs at the farther end of the field. "Ugh!" said she to herself, "Ugh! I must decide what to do before they see that I am awake." She lay there and tried to think what her mother, who came of a very fine family, had told her before she left. "If you have nobody to play with," her mother had said, "don't stop to think about it, and don't act as though you cared. Have a good time by yourself and you will soon have company. If you cannot enjoy yourself, you must not expect others to enjoy you."

"That is what I will do," exclaimed the White Pig. "My mother always gives her children good advice when they go out into the world, and she is right when she says that Pigs of fine family should have fine manners. I will never forget that I am a Yorkshire. I'm glad I didn't say anything mean."

So the White Pig rooted in the sunshine and wallowed in the warm brown earth that she had stirred up with her pink snout. Once in a while she would run to the fence to watch somebody in the lane, and before she knew it she was grunting contentedly to herself. "Really," she said, "I am almost having a good time. I will keep on making believe that I would rather do this than anything else."

* * * * *

The big sister of the Brown Pigs looked over to the White Pig and said, "She's having lots of fun all by herself, it seems to me."

Big brother raised his head. "Let's call her over here," he answered.

"Oh, do!" cried the twelve little Pigs, wriggling their tails. "She looks so full of fun."

"Call her yourself," said the big sister to the big brother.

"Ugh!" called he. "Ugh! Ugh! Don't you want to come over with us, White Pig?"

You can imagine how the White Pig felt when she heard this; how her small eyes twinkled and the corners of her mouth turned up more than ever. She was just about to scamper over and root with them, when she remembered something else that her mother had told her: "Never run after other Pigs. Let them run after you. Then they will think more of you."

She called back, "I'm having too good a time here to leave my rooting-ground. Won't you come over here?"

"Come on," cried all the little Pigs to each other. "Beat you there!"

They ate and talked and slept together all afternoon, and

when the Brown Hog called her children home, they and the White Pig were the best of friends. "Just think," they said to their mother, "the White Pig let us visit her, and she is just as nice as she can be."

The White Pig in her corner of the pen heard this and smiled to herself. "My mother was right," she said; "'Have a good time alone, and everybody will want to come.'"

THE KITTEN WHO LOST HERSELF

"I think," said the Blind Horse, "that something is the matter with my ears." He and the Dappled Gray had been doing field-work all the morning, and were now eating a hearty dinner in their stalls. They were the only people on the first floor of the barn. Even the stray Doves who had wandered in the open door were out in the sunshine once more. Once in a while the whirr of wings told that some Swallow darted through the window into the loft above and flew to her nest under the roof. There was a deep and restful quiet in the sun-warmed air, and yet the Blind Horse had seemed to be listening to something which the other did not hear.

The Dappled Gray stopped eating at once. "Your ears?" said he. "What is wrong with them? I thought your hearing was very good."

"It always has been," was the answer, "and finer than ever since I lost my sight. You know it is always so with us blind people. We learn to hear better than we could before losing our sight. But ever since we came in from the field I have had a queer sound in my ears, and I think there is something the matter with them."

The Dappled Gray stopped eating and stood perfectly still to listen. He did not even switch his tail, although at that minute there were three Flies on his left side and one on his neck. He was trying as hard as he could to hear the queer sound also, for if he did, it would prove that the noise was real and that the Blind Horse's hearing was all right.

He could not hear a thing. "What is it like?" he asked.

"Like the loud purring of a Cat," was the answer, "but everybody knows that the Cat is not purring anywhere around here."

"She might be," said the Dappled Gray. "Where does the sound seem to be?"

"Above my head," said the Blind Horse; "and she certainly would not be purring up there at this time. She would either be sound asleep, or off hunting, or else out in the sunshine, where she loves to sit."

The Dappled Gray felt that this was so, and he could not say a word. He was very sorry for his friend. He thought how dreadful it would seem to be both blind and deaf, and he choked on the oats he was swallowing.

"Now don't worry," said the Blind Horse; "if I should be deaf, I could still feel the soft touch of the breeze on my skin, and could taste my good food, and rub noses with my friends. I wouldn't have spoken of it, only I hoped that you could hear the noise also, and then I would know that it was real." That was just like him. He was always patient and sweet-tempered. In all the years he had been blind, he had never once complained of it, and many times when the other Horses were about to say or do some ill-natured thing, they thought of him and stopped. They were ashamed to be impatient when they were so much better off than he.

The Horses kept on eating their oats and resting from their hard work. In the hay-loft above their heads, the Cat lay and purred and purred and purred, never dreaming that her doing so made trouble for her friends downstairs.

She had been hunting all the night before, creeping softly through the barn and hiding behind bags and boxes to watch for careless Mice and young Rats. They were night-runners as well as she, and many things happened in the barn and farmyard while the larger four-legged people were sound asleep and the fowls were dreaming with their heads tucked under their wings. Sometimes there were not so many Mice in the morning as there had been the evening before, and when this was so, the Cat would walk slowly through the barn and look for a comfortable resting-place. When she found it, she would turn around three times, as her great-great-great-great-great-great-grandmother used to do to trample a bed in the jungle, and then lie down for a long nap. She said she always slept better when her stomach was full, and that was the habit of all Cats.

Sometimes she hunted in the fields, and many a morning at sunrise the Cows had seen her walking toward the barn on the top of the fences. She did not like to wet her feet on the dewy grass when it could be helped; so, as soon as she was through hunting, she jumped on to the nearest fence and went home in that way.

Yes, last night she had been hunting, yet she was not thinking of it now. Neither was she asleep. A Rat gnawed at the boards near her, and she hardly turned her head. A Mouse ran across the floor in plain sight, and she watched him without moving. What did she care about them now? Her first Kittens lay on the hay beside her, and she would not leave them on this first day of their lives unless she really had to.

Of course she had seen little Kittens before—Kittens

that belonged to other Cats—but she was certain that none of them had looked at all like her three charming babies. She could not decide which one of them was the most beautiful. She was a Tortoise-shell Cat herself, and her fur was spotted with white, black, and yellow. The babies had the same colors on their soft coats, but not in just the same way as hers.

At first she thought her largest daughter was the beauty of the family; she was such a clear yellow, with not a hair of any other color on her. "I always did like yellow Cats," said the young mother, "and they are said to be very strong."

Then she looked at her smaller daughter, who was white with tiny yellow and black spots on neck and head. "Such a clean-looking baby," she exclaimed, "and I am sure that when her eyes are open I shall find them blue like my own."

Just at this moment, the warm, dark little bunch of fur between her forepaws moved, and she looked lovingly down upon him, her only son. "He is certainly a very remarkable one," she said. "I never before saw such a fine mixture of yellow and black, first a hair of one and then a hair of the other, so that, unless one is very close to him it looks like a rich brown. And then his feet!" She gave him a loving little poke with one forefoot and turned him onto his back. This made him wave his tiny paws in the air. The thick cushions of skin on each were as black as black could be, and that is very uncommon. They are usually pink, like those of his sisters.

The little fellow lay there, wriggling very feebly, until his mother gave him another poke that turned him over. Then he stretched and crawled toward her, reaching his head first one way and then another. He was so weak that he could not raise his body from the hay, but dragged it along by taking short and uncertain steps with his four shaking legs. It was only a short time since he found that he had legs, and he hadn't any idea how to use them. He just moved whichever one seemed most in his way.

He didn't know where he was going, or what he was going for, but his little stomach was empty and he was cold. Something, he didn't know what, made him drag himself toward the big, warm creature near by. When his black nose touched the fur of her body, he stopped pushing ahead and began to feel from side to side. He did not know now for what he was feeling, yet when he found something his tiny mouth closed around it and a stream of sweet warm milk began to flow down his throat and into his empty stomach. He did not know that it was milk. He did not know anything except that it was good, and then he fell asleep. His sisters did in the same way, and soon the happy mother could look down and see her three babies in a row beside her, all sound asleep. Their pointed little tails lay straight out behind them, and their soft ears were bent forward close to their heads.

"I wonder," said she, "if I was ever as small as they are, and if my mother loved me as I love them." She stretched out one of her forepaws and looked at it. It was so much larger, so very much larger, than the paws of the Kittens. Such a soft and dainty paw as it was, and so perfectly clean. She stretched it even more, and saw five long, curved, sharp claws slide out of their sheaths or cases. She quickly slid them back into their sheaths, for fear that in some way they might happen to touch and hurt her babies.

A Swallow flew down from his nest and passed over her

head, then out of the open window. "Kittens!" said he. "Kittens!" He flew over the fields and saw two Horses standing by the fence while the farmer was oiling his machine. "We have new neighbors in the barn," said he, "and the Cat is purring louder than ever."

"Who are the neighbors?" asked the Dappled Gray.

"Kittens!" sang the Swallow. "Oh, tittle-ittle-ittle-ee."

The Blind Horse drew a long breath. "Then I did hear her purr," said he; "I am so glad." He never made a fuss about his troubles, for he was brave and unselfish, yet the Dappled Gray knew without being told how much lighter his heart was since he heard that the Cat had really been purring above his head.

The days passed by, and the Kittens grew finely. They got their eyes open, first in narrow cracks, and then wider and wider, until they were round and staring. The White Kitten had blue ones, the others brown. In the daytime, they had long, narrow black spots in the middle of their eyes, and as the bright light faded, these black spots spread out sideways until they were quite round. When it was very dark, these spots glowed like great Fireflies in the night. Then the Mice, who often scampered through the loft when the Cat was away, would see three pairs of eyes glowing in the hay, and they would squeak to each other: "See! The Kittens are watching us."

And the Kittens, who were not yet old enough to go hunting, and who were afraid of everything that stirred, would crowd up against each other, arch their little backs, raise their pointed tails, stand their fur on end, and say, "Pst! Ha-a-ah!"

Sometimes they did this when there was not a person in sight and what frightened them was nothing but a wisp of hay, blown down by the wind. Afterward, when anything moved, they sprang at it, held it down with their sharp little claws, and chewed on it with their pointed white teeth. When they were tired of this game, they played hide-and-seek, and when they were tired of that they chased their tails. It was so nice always to have playthings with them. Sometimes, too, they chased each other's tails, and caught them and bit them hard, until the Kitten who owned the tail cried, "Mieow!" and tumbled the biter over.

They were allowed to play all through the loft except over the mangers. Their mother was afraid that if they went there they would fall through the holes which had been left in the floor. During the winter, the farmer used to throw hay down through these to the hungry Horses. When the Cat saw her children going toward these places, she called them back and scolded them. Sometimes she struck them lightly on the ears with her forepaw. "I don't like to," said she, "but they must learn to keep away. It is not safe for them to go there."

One morning when she was away, they were playing hide-and-seek, and the White Kitten was hunting for a good hiding-place. "I'll hide near one of these holes," she said, "and they won't dare come there to look. Then, after they have hunted a long, long time, I'll get another place and let them find me." She did hide there, and after a long, long time, when her brother and sister were in the farther end of the loft, she tried to run over to another dark corner. Instead of that, the hay began to slip and slide under her and she went down, down, down, through a long dark box, and hit with a hard thud at the bottom.

She was so scared that she couldn't have told how many toes she had on her forefeet. Of course, she had five on each, like all Kittens, and four on each hind-foot, but if anybody had asked her then, she would have been quite likely to say "three."

She was sore, too, and when she felt a warm breath on her and opened her eyes, she saw that some great creature had thrust his nose through a hole in the side of the dark box. "It must be a Horse," she thought, "and my mother says that they are kind to Cats. I think I'd better tell him who I am. I don't want him to take me for a Pig, because he may not like Pigs." You see, she forgot that Horses had been living in the great world and could tell to what family a person belonged the very first time they saw him. The only people she had ever seen were Swallows and Mice.

"If—if you please, sir," she said, "I am the White Kitten, and I just tumbled down from the hay-loft, but I didn't mean to."

"I am the Blind Horse," answered a strong and gentle voice outside, "and I hope you are not hurt."

"Not very much," answered the Kitten. "I just feel ache-y in my back and scared all over."

"Come out into the manger, White Kitten," said the Blind Horse, "and perhaps you won't be so scared. I won't touch you, although I should like to. You know I am blind, and so, unless I can touch people I don't know how they look."

The White Kitten crawled out and saw him, and then she wasn't afraid at all. She was so sorry for him that she

couldn't be afraid. She remembered the time before her eyes opened when she had to feel for everything she wanted. It was not so hard then, because she did not know anything different, but now she could not bear to think of not being able to see all that was around her. "If you will put your nose down in the other end of the manger," she said, "I will rub up against it, and you will know more how I look."

The Blind Horse did this, and who can tell how happy it made him when her warm and furry back rubbed up against his nose? "Thank you," he whinnied; "you are very good."

"Would you know I was a Kitten if I hadn't told you?" she said.

"Indeed I would," he answered.

"And you wouldn't have thought me a Pig?" she asked.

"Never!" said he; "I wouldn't even have believed you if you had told me that you were one."

The Blind Horse and the White Kitten became firm friends, and when she tried to wash off the dirt that got into her fur she sat in the very middle of the manger and told him all about it.

"My mother always has washed me," she said, "but my tongue is getting big enough to wash with now. It is getting rougher, too, and that is a good thing. My mother says that the reason why all the prickles on Cats' tongues point backward is because then we can lick all the meat off from bones with them. I'm 'most old enough to eat meat now. I can't wash the top of my head though. You have to wet your paw and scrub it with that. Can you wash the top of your head?"

Then the Blind Horse told her how the men kept him

clean; and while he was telling this the Cat came into his stall, crying and looking for her child.

"Oh, mother," cried the White Kitten, "I tumbled down, but I didn't mean to, and I'm sorry I didn't mind you, and the Blind Horse can't wash the top of his head, and he knew that I wasn't a Pig."

The Cat was so glad to find the White Kitten that she didn't scold at all, but jumped into the manger and washed her clean, and then caught the loose skin of the Kitten's neck between her teeth and carried her through the stalls, across the barn-floor, and up the stairs to their home. That made the Kitten much ashamed, for she thought that she was old enough to go alone.

For two whole days after this the White Kitten was so lame from her fall that she could only lie still on the hay, and she could see that her mother did not treat her as before. "I won't ever go near those places again," she said. "I never will."

"You promised me before that you would stay away," said her mother, "and you broke your promise." She did not punish the White Kitten, but she felt very sad and she could not help showing it. There was a dreadful ache in her child's little Kitten-heart that was a great deal worse than the lameness in her back or in her neck or in her legs.

At last there came a day when the whole family walked downstairs, and the Cat showed her three children to the farmyard people and spoke a few words about each. "The yellow Kitten, my big daughter," said she, "promises to be the best hunter: she is a wonderful jumper, and her claws are already nearly as long as mine. My son, the brown one, has a remarkable voice. And this White Kitten, my little daughter, is the most obedient of all. She has never disobeyed me since the day she fell into the manger, and I can trust her perfectly."

Then the White Kitten knew that she was quite forgiven, and she was the happiest person on the farm.

THE CHICKEN WHO WOULDN'T EAT GRAVEL

It was some time after the Dorking Hen had come off the nest with her little brood, that the mother of the Shanghai Chickens began to have so much trouble.

She had twelve as fine Chickens as you could find anywhere: tall, wide-awake youngsters with long and shapely legs and thick down and feathers. She was very proud of them, as any Hen mother might well be, and often said to the Shanghai Cock, "Did you ever see so fine a family? Look at those twenty-four legs, all so long and straight, and not a feather on one of them." His eyes would shine and he would stretch his neck with pride, but all he ever said to her was, "They will do very well if they only behave as well as they look." He did not believe in praising children to their faces, and he thought their mother spoiled them.

Perhaps he was right, for the little Shanghais soon found out that they were good-looking, and they wanted everybody in the poultry-yard to notice their legs. It was very foolish, of course, to be proud of such things, but when the other fowls said, "We should think you would be cold without feathers on your legs," they answered, "Oh, we are Shanghais, and our family never wear feathers there!" And that was true, just as it is true that the Dorkings have extra toes, and that the Black Spanish fowls have white ears.

The Shanghai mother was now roaming the fields with her brood, and there was rich picking in the wheat-stubble. All the fowls were out of the yard now, and would not be shut up until cold weather. Early in the morning they would start out in parties of from six to a dozen, with a Cock at the head of each. He chose the way in which they should go; he watched the sky for Hawks, and if he saw one, gave a warning cry that made the Hens hurry to him. The Cocks are the lords of the poultry-yard and say how things shall be there; but when you see them leading the way in the fields,—ah, then you know why all the fowls obey them.

The farmyard people still tell of the day when a Hawk swooped down on one of the young Dorkings and would have carried him off if the Black Spanish Cock had not jumped out, and pecked him and struck at him with his spurs, and fought, until the Hawk was glad to hurry away. The Cocks are not only brave—they are polite, too, and when they find food they will not eat it until they have called the Hens to come and share with them.

You can imagine what good times the Chickens had in the stubble-fields. They were so old now that their down was all covered with feathers, and some of them wondered if they couldn't feel their spurs growing. Still, that was all nonsense, as a Bantam told them, because spurs do not start until the fowl is a year old. They had long been too large to cuddle under their mother's feathers at night, and had taken their first lessons in roosting before they went to the stubble-fields. They had learned to break up their own food, too, and that was a great help to their mother. Fowls, you know, have no teeth, and no matter how big a mouthful one takes he has to swallow it whole. The only way they can help themselves is to break the pieces apart with their feet or peck them apart with their bills before eating them.

The yellow grains of wheat that lay everywhere in the field were fine food, and should have made the little Shanghais as fat as the Grouse who sometimes stole out from the edge of the forest. Eleven of the brood were quite plump, but one Chicken was still thin and lank. His mother was very much worried about him and could not think what was the matter. She spoke of it to the Black Spanish Hen one day, but the Black Spanish Hen had never raised a brood, and said she really didn't know any more about the care of Chickens than if she were a Dove. Then the anxious mother went to the Shanghai Cock about it. He listened to all she said and looked very knowing.

"I don't think there is anything the matter," said he. "The Chick is growing fast, that is all. I remember how it was with me before I got my long tail-feathers. I was very thin, yet see what a fine-looking fellow I am now." He was really a sight worth seeing as he towered above the other fowls, flapping his strong wings in the sunshine and crowing. His feathers were beautiful, and the bright red of his comb and wattles showed that he was well. "Ah," thought the Shanghai Hen, "if my Chicken could only become such a fine-looking Cock!" And she didn't worry any more all day.

That night she and her brood roosted in the old apple-tree in the corner of the orchard nearest the poultry-yard. She flew up with the older fowls and fluttered and lurched and squawked and pushed on first one branch and then another, while the Chickens were walking up a slanting board that the farmer had placed against one of the lower branches. It always takes fowls a long time to settle themselves for the night. They change places and push each other, and sometimes one sleepy Hen leans over too far and falls to the ground, and then has to begin all over again.

At first the Chickens had feared that they would tumble off as soon as they were asleep, but they soon learned that their feet and the feet of all other birds are made in such a way that they hang on tightly even during sleep. The weight of the bird's body above hooks the toes around the branch, and there they stay until the bird wishes to unhook them.

After a long time, all the fowls were asleep with their heads under their wings. The Sheep, Pigs, and Cows were dreaming, and even the Horses were quiet in their stalls. There was not a light to be seen in the big white farmhouse, when the Dorking Cock crowed in his sleep. That awakened him and all the other fowls as well. Then the other Cocks crowed because he did and he crowed again because they did, and they crowed again because he had crowed again, and the Chickens asked if it were not almost morning, and their mothers told them not to talk but to go to sleep at once and make morning come more quickly.

All of this took quite a while, and the Shanghai mother could not sleep again. She could see her brood quite plainly in the moonlight, and one of them was not plump like the rest. She roosted there and worried about him until suddenly (she could never tell how it happened) she seemed to know just what was the matter.

She flew down beside him and poked him under his

wing. "Wake up," she said. "I want to ask you something. Do you eat gravel?"

"No," he answered sleepily, "I don't like gravel."

"Didn't I bring you up to eat it?" she asked sternly.

"Yes, but I don't like it, and now that I am old enough to roost in a tree I don't mean to eat any more. So!"

Just imagine a Chicken talking to his mother in that way! His mother, who had laid the egg from which he was hatched; who had sat upon the nest through all the weary days and nights while he was growing inside his shell; who had cuddled him under her soft feathers; who had taught him all he knew, and would have fought any hawk to save him! She had begun to love him before he even knew that he was, and had lived for him and his brother and sisters ever since.

The mother said nothing more to him then. She spent the rest of the night watching the stars and the moon and the first rosy flush of the eastern sky which told that morning was near. Then she said to her naughty Chicken, as he began to stir and cheep, "I shall never try to make you eat gravel if you think you are too big to mind your mother. I shall just tell you this, that you will never be strong unless you do. I have not told you why, because you never asked, and I supposed you would do as you ought without knowing the reason. You have no teeth, and you cannot chew the grain you eat before it is swallowed. You have a strong stomach, and if you eat gravel this stomach or gizzard will rub and press the tiny stones against the grain until it is well broken up and ready to make into fat and strength for your body."

"But it doesn't taste good," he replied, "and I'd rather

eat other things. I don't believe it matters, and I won't eat it anyway."

The Shanghai Hen flew down from the tree and clucked to her Chickens. She would not waste time talking to him. Whenever he came near her that day, he ate everything but gravel. He had his own way and yet he was not happy. For some reason, nothing seemed to be any fun. Even lying under the bushes on the sunshiny side was not comfortable, and when he wallowed in the dust with his brothers and sisters he didn't enjoy that.

Things went on this way for a good many days, and at last he saw that his shadow was only a small black spot on the ground, while his brothers and sisters had big fat shadows. He heard the Black Spanish Cock call him a Bantam, and the Shanghai Cock say that he wouldn't live until his spurs grew. One of the Dorking Chickens was talking to her sister, and he heard her say, "Imagine him at the head of a flock!" Then she laughed, a mean, cackling little laugh.

That night, when the rest were asleep in the apple-tree, he walked softly down the slanting board and ate gravel. The next morning he felt better than he had in a long time, so when there was nobody around he ate some more. He didn't want anyone else to know that he had found out his mistake. Every morning he looked at his shadow, and it grew fatter and fatter. Still he was not happy, and he knew it was because he had not told his patient old mother. He wanted to tell her, too. One day he heard her telling his brother to eat more gravel, and the brother said he didn't like the taste of it. That made him speak at last.

"Suppose you don't like it, you can eat it. Queer world

it would be if we didn't have to do unpleasant things. I've just made up my mind that the people who won't do hard things, when they ought to, have the hardest times in the end. Wish I'd minded my mother and eaten gravel when she told me to, and I'm not going to let you be as foolish as I was."

Just then he heard somebody say of him, "What a fine-looking fellow he is growing to be! I like him ever so much now."

It was the Dorking Chicken who had laughed at him. He ran after a Grasshopper, and she ran after the same Grasshopper, and they ran against each other and the Grasshopper got away, so of course they had to wander off together to find something to eat, and after that they became great friends.

The Shanghai Hen looked lovingly after him and raised one foot in the air. "Now," she said, "I am perfectly happy."

THE GOOSE WHO WANTED HER OWN WAY

It would be hard to tell which family is the most important among the farmyard people. There is no one animal so wise as Collie, the farmer's dog, and all the rest love him and mind him when he is sent to bring them up from the pasture or to drive them to the water. Still, he does not spend his days in barn or field and only comes with his master or for a visit now and then.

You may remember how the Garter Snake and the old Tree Frog were the leaders in the meadow, and how in the forest all looked up to the Ground Hog. These people were patient and old, and partly because they were old and had had many years in which to think about life, they were very wise. In the farmyard the Oxen were the most patient and the oldest, and it was to them that all the animals went when they were in trouble.

There were also the Horses, fine strong creatures, always helping somebody else and working all day during most of the year. They drew the reaper through the tall grain, and where in the morning had been a field of waving golden wheat, at sunset were bundles or sheaves of gathered grain, and the stubble was ready for the fowls. They were busy people; and sometimes during the winter they liked to remind their neighbors how much they had done.

Then again, there were the Cows, who are the sisters of

the Oxen. They are large and there are many of them, yet they are not so wise, and that is easily understood. All that they have to do on the farm is to give milk for the butter-and cheese-making, and for the farmer's children to drink. No farmer could get along without his Cows, but they do not work like their brothers. They have so easy a time that they do not learn much. You know, when people work, they have to think, and when people think enough useful thoughts it makes them wise. That is one of the many reasons why it is so foolish to be lazy.

Truly, it would be hard to say which farmyard family is the most important, but there is no trouble at all in telling which family think themselves the most so. If you ask any Goose, she will tell you that one of their flock is worth five Horses or a dozen Cows. Nobody else would tell you this, and if you should speak of it to the span of Bays, or the Dappled Gray, or even the youngest Colt in the stable, they would answer you only with a hearty Horse laugh. The Cows would smile and reply, "What a Goose she was to say that!"

There has always been a flock of Geese on the farm, and their neighbors are so used to their queer ways that they only smile when the Geese put on airs, and it is a good-natured smile, too. They even feel rather sorry for them when they lose their feathers, although the Nigh Ox once said that if it were not for being plucked once in a while, the Geese would really be too airy to live with.

Perhaps the Nigh Ox was right in what he said, for certainly after they have worn their feathers all winter, they hold their heads higher than ever, and tell what they think and what they would do, and it is well they should be reminded that they work for a living like all their neighbors. The farmer's wife never plucks the Geese until warm weather comes. Then she takes all the soft, short feathers that they have worn through the winter, and this leaves them looking very ragged indeed. There was a time, years ago, when Geese had to give up their long tail-and wing-feathers to be whittled into pens, but these Geese didn't know about that, and there was nobody in the farmyard old enough to remember it and tell them, so they thought they had a pretty hard time in even giving up their breast feathers.

"Sssss!" the Gander used to say, "if the farmer's boys must have feather pillows on which to lay their heads, why do they not grow their own feathers?"

"Humph!" said the Nigh Ox once; "If you must have oats to eat, why don't you grow the oats?" But the Gander was already waddling away and pretended not to hear him.

It is in the winter that the Geese put on the most airs. Then, when the Horses are being harnessed, they say to each other, "Dear me! Wouldn't it be dreadful to work in that way for a living?" And sometimes, when the team is hitched to a post by the farmhouse, they waddle past in a single line with the Gander at the head, and say to the Horses: "Hear you have to take a load of wood to town. It's too bad. Hope you won't get very tired. We are going to the river for a nice cold swim. Good-bye." Then they march off with their heads held high, and as soon as their backs are turned, the Horses look at each other and laugh softly. They know that there is nothing in the world better than good, honest, hard work, no matter of what kind it is.

Every winter the Geese forget about having to be

plucked, and every spring they are surprised to lose their feathers. They are plucked four times before fall comes, and these four times come so near together that even they can remember from one to another. You would think that then they would not be so airy, but instead of saying, "Of course we work for our living—why shouldn't we?" they say, "Why, yes, we do let the farmer's wife have some of our feathers when she wants them. We suppose you might call it work to grow feathers for her, still it does not take much of our time, and it is quite different from drawing loads and getting tired as the Horses and Oxen do. Growing feathers is genteel."

They do not remember anything long, and so, when they have made a mistake once, they are likely to make the same mistake over and over again. Then, too, they cannot tell big things from little things, and they are not happy unless they can have their own way all the time. And you know that nobody can be sure of that. It all comes of their not being willing to think hard, and sometimes it makes them a great deal of trouble, as it did on the day when the Gray Goose would not go through the farmyard gate.

This was soon after the Gander and his wife had hatched their brood of seven Goslings, and they were taking them at once to the brook. It was a happy day for all the flock. The Gander and the Mother Goose were glad because their children were safely out of the shell, and because they would no longer have to sit with cramped legs on the nest. Ganders are good fathers, for they cover the eggs half of the time, while the Mother Goose is resting. The other Geese were not only proud of the Goslings, but they were glad to have

the Gander and the Mother Goose free to go around with them again. They had missed them very much.

The gate from the farmyard into the meadow stood wide open, and all the Geese except the Gray one followed the Gander through. The Gray Goose tried to go through a small hole in the fence very near the gate. She squeezed her head into it and stretched her neck on the meadow side of the fence, but she could not get any farther, although she pushed until she was dizzy.

"Wait for me," she cried. "Wait for me-ee!"

"Hurry, then," said the Gander.

"I am hurrying," she cried, and she pushed with all her strength, but since the hole in the fence was so small, she did not get any farther than before.

"Go through the gateway," said the Nigh Ox, who was grazing near by.

"Sssss!" said the Gray Goose stiffly. "I would rather go through here. I have chosen to go this way."

"Oh!" said the Nigh Ox, "excuse me! Do go through there by all means!"

"We are going on," called the Gander; "we would wait, but the Goslings are in a hurry to take their first bath. Come as soon as you can."

The Gray Goose tried harder than ever to go the way that she had chosen, but it only made her so out of breath that she had to lie down and rest. Once she thought she heard somebody laugh, yet when she looked at the Nigh Ox, who was the only person around, he was lying with closed eyes and solemnly chewing his cud, so she decided that she must have been mistaken.

Down by the brook the rest of the flock were cackling merrily, and she could see the seven Goslings swimming with the Geese and the Gander. "Oh," she cried, "how I wish I were with them! I don't see what is the matter with this hole in the fence. The farmer ought to make it bigger."

She pushed and scolded and fussed until her neck was sore and she was too tired to swim if she had a chance, so she sat down to rest. She did remember what the Nigh Ox had said; still, if she couldn't go as she had planned, she wouldn't go at all. She walked into the barn to find a cool and shady place, lowering her head as she stepped over the threshold of the high front door.

"What did you do that for?" twittered a Swallow.

"Because I don't want to hit my head on the top of the doorway;" she replied. "I always do so. All of our flock do so."

"Tittle-ittle-ittle-ee," laughed the Swallow, as she darted away and alighted on the fence by the Nigh Ox. "Why isn't the Gray Goose in swimming with the rest?" asked she.

"Because she can't push her fat body through that hole in the fence," said the Nigh Ox, switching his tail toward it as he spoke.

"Why doesn't she go through the gateway, then?" asked the Swallow.

"Because she says she would rather go the other way, and that if she can't go that way, she won't go at all."

"And she is missing all that fun?" said the Swallow.

"All of it," answered the Nigh Ox, "but then, you know, she is such a Goose!"

WHY THE SHEEP RAN AWAY

It was during the hottest summer weather that the wind-storm came. The farmyard people always spoke of it as "the" wind-storm, because not even the Blind Horse, who had lived on the farm longer than any of his neighbors, could remember anything like it. "I recall one time," he said, "when a sweet-apple tree was blown down in the fall. The Hogs found it and ate all the fruit before the farmer knew that it was down. You should have heard them grunt over it. They were afraid the farmer would drive them away before they had eaten it all. Eh, well! They ate all they wanted, but one of the Pigs told me afterward that it made them sick, and that he never wanted to see another sweet apple as long as he lived. That was a hard storm, but not like this, not like this."

It had come in the night when the farmyard people were asleep, and there was much scampering to shelter. The fowls, who were roosting in the old apple-tree, did not have time to oil their feathers and make them water-proof. They just flew off their perches as fast as they could and ran for the open door of the Hen-house. When they were once inside, they ruffled up their feathers and shook themselves to get rid of the rain-drops. Fowls do not like wet weather, and it vexes them very much to be in the rain. Their neighbors know this so well that it has become their custom to say of an angry person that he is "as mad as a wet Hen."

The Cows were in their part of the barn with their necks between the stanchions, so there was nothing for them to do but to keep still and think of those who were out of doors. The Horses were in their comfortable stalls. They had been working hard all day and the farmer had gotten a good supper of oats ready for them in their mangers, so that they could eat quickly and go to sleep, instead of staying awake and walking around to get their own suppers in the pasture.

Out in the meadow the Sheep huddled close together under a low-branching tree, and stood still until the storm passed. They had been so warm that the cool rain made them comfortable, but the wind pushed them and swayed the branches of the trees. The loud thunder made the Lambs jump. They liked the lightning and made a game out of it, each one telling what he had seen by the last flash. The clouds, too, were beautiful, and flew across the sky like great dark birds with downy breasts, dropping now and then shining worms from their beaks.

At last the air became cool and clear, and the clouds flew far away toward the east. Next, the stars peeped out, first one, then two, then six, then twenty, and then so many that you could not have counted them,—more than the leaves on a maple-tree, more than the grass-blades of the meadow. The Sheep ran around a little to shake off the rain-drops and warm themselves, then they huddled down again to sleep.

When the sun arose in the eastern sky, his warm beams fell upon the Sheep and awakened them. "How cool and beautiful a day," they said. "What a morning for a run!"

"I can beat you to the tall grass!" called one little Lamb to the rest, and they all scampered around the field, throwing up their heels for joy. They had been away from their mothers for awhile, and had learned to eat grass instead of milk. They were quite proud of the way in which they broke it off, with quick upward jerks of their heads, and their teeth were growing finely. They did not expect any upper front teeth, for in place of them the Sheep have only a hard pad of flesh.

Soon they came running back to the flock. "There is a Dog over there," they cried, "a strange Dog. He doesn't look like Collie. He is coming this way, and we are afraid."

Their uncle, the Bell-Wether, looked over to where the strange Dog was, then turned quickly and began to run. The bell around his neck clinked at every step. When the other Sheep heard the bell they raised their heads and ran after him, and the Lambs ran after them. The strange Dog did not follow or even bark at them, yet on they went, shaking the shining rain-drops from the grass as they trod upon it. Not one of them was thinking for himself what he really ought to do. The Bell-Wether thought, "I feel like running away from the Dog, and so I will run."

The other Sheep said to themselves, "The Bell-Wether is running and so we will run."

And the Lambs said, "If they are all running we will run."

Along the fence they went, the bell clinking, their hoofs pattering, and not one of them thinking for himself, until they reached a place where the fence was blown over. It was not blown 'way down, but leaned so that it could be jumped. If a single one of the flock, even the youngest Lamb, had said, "Don't jump!" they would have stayed in the pasture; but nobody said it. The Bell-Wether felt like jumping over, so he jumped. Then the Sheep did as the Bell-Wether had done, and the Lambs did as the Sheep had done.

Now they were in the road and the Bell-Wether turned away from the farmhouse and ran on, with the Sheep and the Lambs following. Even now, if anybody had said, "Stop!" they would have stopped, for they knew that they were doing wrong; but nobody said it.

After a while a heavy wagon came rumbling down the road behind them, and the Bell-Wether jumped over a ditch and ran into a hilly field with woodland beyond. Because he went the Sheep did, and because the Sheep went the Lambs did, and nobody said "Stop!" You see, by this time they were very badly frightened, and no wonder. When they saw the strange Dog they were a little scared, for they thought he might chase them. If they had made themselves stay there and act brave they would soon have felt brave. Even if the Dog had been a cruel one, they could have kept him from hurting them, for Sheep have been given very strong, hard foreheads with which to strike, and the Bell-Wether had also long, curled horns with three ridges on the side of each. But it is with Sheep as it is with other people,—if they let themselves be frightened they grow more and more fearful, even when there is no real danger and now all of their trouble came from their not stopping to think what they ought to do.

They hurried up to the highest ground in the field, and when they were there and could go no farther, they stopped and looked at each other. One Lamb said to his mother,

"Why did we come here? It isn't nearly so nice as our own meadow."

"Why, I came because the Bell-Wether did," she answered. Then she turned to the Bell-Wether and said, "Why did you bring us here?"

"I didn't bring you here," he replied. "I felt like coming, and I came. I didn't make you follow."

"N-no," answered the Sheep; "but you might have known that if you came the Sheep would come."

"Well," said the Bell-Wether, "you might have known that if you Sheep came the Lambs would, so you'd better not say anything."

"Baa!" cried the Lambs. "We are hot and thirsty and there isn't any water here to drink. We want to go back."

Everybody was out of patience with somebody else, and nobody was comfortable. They did not dare try to go home again, for fear they would have more trouble, so they huddled together on the top of the hill and were very miserable and unhappy. They hadn't any good reason for coming, and they could not even have told why they ran to the hilltop instead of staying in the pleasant hollow below.

There was a reason for their running up, however, although they didn't know it. It was because their great-great-great-great-great-great-grandfather and-grandmother were wild Sheep in the mountains, and when frightened ran up among the rocks where there was nobody to hurt them. They got into the habit of running up-hill when scared, and their children did the same, and their children's children did the same, and now even the farmyard Sheep do so, although they long ago forgot the reason why.

"Bow-wow-wow!" rang out on the still morning air.

"There's Collie!" cried the Lambs joyfully. "He's coming to take us home. Let's bleat to help him find us more quickly." All the Lambs said, "Baa! Baaa!" in their high, soft voices, and their mothers said "Baa! Baaa!" more loudly; and the Bell-Wether added his "Baa! Baaa!" which was so deep and strong that it sounded like a little, very little, clap of thunder.

Collie came frisking along with his tail waving and his eyes gleaming. He started the flock home, and scolded them and made fun of them all the way, but they were now so happy that they didn't care what he said. When they were safely in the home meadow again and the farmer had mended the fence, Collie left them. As he turned to go, he called back one last piece of advice.

"I'm a Shepherd Dog," he said, "and it's my work to take care of Sheep when they can't take care of themselves, but I'd just like to be a Bell-Wether for a little while. You wouldn't catch me doing every foolish thing I felt like doing and getting all the flock into trouble by following me! Nobody can do anything without somebody else doing it too, and I wouldn't lead people into trouble and then say I didn't think. Bow-wow-wow-wow!"

The Bell-Wether grumbled to himself, "Well, the rest needn't tag along unless they want to. Pity if I can't jump a fence without everybody following." But down in his heart he felt mean, for he knew that one who leads should do right things.

THE FINE YOUNG RAT AND THE TRAP

THE Mice were having a great frolic in the corn-crib. The farmer's man had carelessly left a board leaning up against it in such a way that they could walk right up and through one of the big cracks in the side. It was the first time that some of them had ever been here. When the farmer built the crib, he had put a tin pan, open side down, on top of each of the wooden posts, and had then nailed the floor beams of the crib through these pans. That had kept the hungry Mice from getting into the corn.

This was a great day for them, and their gnawing-teeth would certainly be worn down enough without giving them any extra wear. That, you know, is one thing about which all Rats and Mice have to be very careful, for their front teeth are growing all the time, and they have to gnaw hard things every day to keep them from becoming too long.

There was only one thing that ever really troubled these Mice, and that was the Cat. They did not feel afraid of Hawks and Owls because they lived indoors. Weasels did not often come up to the barn, and men made so much noise when they were around that any wide-awake Mouse could easily keep out of their way. With the Cat it was different. She was always prowling around in the night-time, just when they had their finest parties; and many a young Mouse had been scared away from a midnight supper by seeing her eyes glowing like balls of fire in the darkness. By daylight it was not so bad, for they could see her coming, and besides, she slept much of the time then.

They were talking about her when in the corn-crib. "Have any of you seen the Cat to-day?" asked the Oldest Mouse.

Nobody answered. Then one young fellow, who was always worrying, said: "Supposing she should come out of the barn now! Supposing she should come right toward this corn-crib! Supposing she should stand right under the floor! Supposing she should catch us as we jumped down! Supposing—"

But here the other young Mice all squeaked to him to stop, and one of them declared that it made her fur stand on end to think of it. The Oldest Mouse spoke quite sharply. "Supposing," said he to the first young Mouse, "you should eat more and talk less. There are enough pleasant things to speak about without scaring all your friends in this way."

The young Mouse who said that her fur stood on end couldn't eat anything more, she was so frightened. "What could we do," she said, "if the Cat should come?"

"Stay right where we are," answered her mother. "She couldn't reach us with the door closed. Now go on with your eating and don't be foolish."

A Rat ran up the board. "Good-morning," said he. "Have you heard the news?"

"No, no!" cried the Mice, hurrying to that side of the corn-crib, and peeping through the crack.

"The Yellow Kitten has been hunting with her mother, and they say that her brother is going to-night."

"Well," said a mother Mouse, "I knew we would have

to expect it, but I did hope they would wait a while. Now, children," she added, "do be careful! I know that when you are looking for food you have to go into dangerous places, but don't stop there to talk or to clean your fur. Find safe corners for that, or I shall worry about you all the time."

"We will," squeaked all the little Mice together. "We will be very, very careful."

"Thank you for the news," said the Oldest Mouse to the Rat. "We will try to send you word of new dangers when we hear of them."

The Rat, who was a fine young fellow, ran down the board and away. They could not ask him in to lunch, because he was too large and stout to squeeze through the cracks, but he understood how it was, and knew that he could find food elsewhere. Now he ran to the Pig-pen to snatch a share of the breakfast which the farmer had just left there. He often did this as soon as the farmer went away, and the Pigs never troubled him. Perhaps that was because they knew that if they drove him away when he came alone, he would bring all his sisters and his cousins and his aunts, and his brothers and his uncles too, the next time, and would eat every bit of food they had.

After he had taken a hearty breakfast, he ran under the edge of the barn to clean himself. He was always very particular about this. His mother had taught him when very small that he must keep his fur well brushed and his face washed, and he did it just as a Cat would, by wetting his paws and scrubbing his face and the top of his head. He brushed his fur coat with his paws also.

While he was here, one of his cousins came from the barn

above. She ran down the inside of the wall, head foremost, and her hind feet were turned around until they pointed backward. That let her hold on with her long, sharp claws, quite as a Squirrel does, and kept her from tumbling. She was much out of breath when she reached the ground, but it was not from running.

"What do you think that farmer has done now?" she cried. "It was bad enough for him to nail tin over the holes we gnawed into his grain-bins, but this is worse still. It needn't make us so much trouble, but it hurts my feelings."

"What is it?" asked her cousin.

"A trap!" said she. "A horrible, shining trap. The Rat from the other farm told me about it. It lies open and flat on the floor of a grain-bin,—the very one you and I gnawed into last night,—and there is a lovely piece of cheese in the middle of it. The Rat who told me about it says that as soon as one touches the cheese, the trap springs shut on him."

"Bah!" exclaimed the young Rat who had just eaten breakfast in the Pig-pen. "Let it stay there! We don't have to touch it, although I do mean to look at it some time. I believe in knowing about things."

"I wish you wouldn't look at it," said his cousin, who was very fond of him.

"The Rat from the other farm says it is very dangerous to even look at traps, especially if your stomach is empty."

"Then the Rat from the other farm might better keep away," said this young fellow, as he put one paw up to see that his whiskers were all right. "I don't think very much of him anyway. He thinks he knows everything because he has travelled. I wish you would have nothing to do with him. I dare say you were in the grain-bin with him when you saw the trap."

"Yes," said she, "I was."

"Well," said he, "you both got away safely, and I shall too. I may not be very clever, but I think I do know enough to keep out of a trap." Then he turned into his hole and went to sleep. He had been running around all night, and was very tired. He was cross, too. This was the second time that his cousin had told him what the Rat from the other farm had said, and he thought she liked him altogether too well.

When he awakened, it was night again and he was aroused by the stamping of the Dappled Gray on the floor above his head. For a minute he could hardly think where he was. Then it all came to him. He was in his own cozy little hole under the barn, and it was night. He remembered something about the Yellow Kitten. What was it? Oh yes, she had begun hunting. Well, he was not afraid of her yet. But there was something else—the trap! He wondered if his cousin were in that bin again. As like as not her friend, the Rat from the other farm, was showing her the trap now. He would go up there himself, and at once, too.

He ran up the wall, through an opening, and across the barn floor to the grain-bin. It was a moonlight night and the barn was not very dark. The cover of the bin was raised. Perhaps the farmer's man had forgotten to close it. Perhaps there was so little grain left in it that the man didn't care to. At any rate, he could now see the trap quite plainly. There was nobody else in the bin, and he went close to it.

"I would not touch it for anything," said he, as he entered the bin, "but it will not hurt me to look at it."

When he went nearer, he was very careful to see that his tail did not even brush against the chain which held the trap down. "So that is the terrible, dangerous trap?" said he. "It doesn't look particularly dreadful. That is fine-smelling cheese though." He sniffed two or three times. "I have tasted cheese only once in my whole life," said he, "and I am almost starved now. I wouldn't mind a nibble at that." He looked at it and thought about it until it seemed to him he could not go away and leave that cheese there.

Then he thought, "If I am very careful to step over these shining steel things and rest my feet only on the floor, it cannot spring the trap. Then I will snatch the cheese and jump.... I am pretty sure I can do it.... Why, yes, I know I can." So the Rat who had come just to look at the trap, began to lift first one foot and then another over the shining curved bars, and got all ready to catch up the cheese and run.

"Now!" he cried. "One, two, three!" He did snatch it and jump, but the trap jumped, too, in its own trappy way, and the Rat who got the cheese left the three tip rings of his tail to pay for it. "Ouch!" he cried. "My tail! My tail! My beautiful, long, bony tail, all covered with scales and short hair!" He did not care at all for the cheese now. He did not want to see it, for he would rather have had the point on his tail again than to eat a whole binful of cheese.

"How it will look!" said he. "So stumpy and blunt. And it has been so very useful always. I could wind it around a stick to hold myself up when my paws were full, and many a time I have rolled eggs across the floor by curling it around them." Then he heard Rat voices and scampered out and down to his own hole.

His cousin and the Rat from the other farm came into the bin. "Don't look at the trap," he was saying, "but just eat your grain from the farther corner."

"I won't," she answered, and she half closed her eyes to keep from seeing it. He was beside her and they stumbled over the cheese, which now lay on the floor away from the trap. "How does this happen?" said he. "We will eat it first and then find out." By this advice he showed that he was a Rat of excellent sense.

When they had eaten it, they began to look toward the trap. As there was no longer any cheese in it to tempt them, they felt perfectly safe in doing so. They found that it had been sprung, and there lay the last three rings of some Rat's tail.

"How dreadful!" she exclaimed. "I hope that was not lost by any of our friends."

"Hum-hum!" said the Rat from the other farm. "Now, whom have I seen wearing that? I have certainly seen that tail before—it was your cousin!"

"Poor fellow!" said she. "I must go to see him."

"Oh, don't go now," cried the Rat from the other farm. "I think he might want to be alone for a while. Besides," he added coaxingly, "you haven't tasted of the grain yet, and it is very good."

"W-well," answered she, "perhaps my cousin would just as soon not have me come now." So she waited, and the Rat from the other farm told her wonderful stories of his travels, and they had a very fine supper.

When her cousin began to run around again, he was a much sadder and wiser Rat. Sometimes the younger Rats would ask him how he lost the tip of his tail. "By not turning it toward a tempting danger," he would answer, very solemnly. Then, after he had told them the story, he always added, "The time to turn your tail toward a tempting danger is the minute you see it, for if you wait and look and long for something you ought not to take, there is sure to be trouble, and many a Rat has lost more than the tip of his tail in just that way."

THE QUICK-TEMPERED TURKEY GOBBLER

THERE was only one Gobbler on the farm, and he was so used to having his own way that he never tried to make the best of it when he couldn't, and sometimes he became exceedingly cross. He was bigger than the Cocks, the Hens, the Geese, and the Ducks, so when they were in his way and he gobbled a gruff "Move along," they murmured "Oh, certainly," and scampered away as fast as their legs would carry them. The Peacock was larger than the Turkey Gobbler, it is true, but as long as he could sit on a fence in the sunshine and have somebody admiring his train, he did not care anything about the Gobbler, and they did not get in each other's way.

There were seven Hen Turkeys, timid, sweet-tempered people, who were fond of walking. They had never been known to answer back when the Gobbler scolded them, although at times he was very unreasonable. This was polite of them, but it made the Gobbler more careless than ever of the way in which he spoke. The Black Spanish Hen said it made her wattles tingle to hear him find fault with them. She wouldn't have stood it—no, indeed!

When the Black Spanish Cock heard her say so, he shook his feathers and smiled a queer little smile, and said, "I certainly know that she would not." The other fowls looked at each other, and the Shanghai Cock winked his round little eyes at the Dorking Hen, and she had to oil a feather on the under side of her wing just then, so, of course, nobody saw her laugh—if she did laugh.

The Black Spanish fowls were kind-hearted and honest, and had fine manners, but they would not stand it to be spoken to hastily by any one who was not very much bigger than they, and it was said that the Cock had once—only once—but then, perhaps it would be just as well not to tell what the other fowls had heard about their family quarrel, for, after all, it did not come very straight, the Pigs having told the Geese, and the Geese telling the Ducks, and the Ducks just mentioning it to the Peacock, and the Peacock having spoken of it to the Dorking Hen.

It was now late in the fall, and all the Turkeys went walking together again. One would think that, after being separated from the rest all summer and part of the spring, the Gobbler would have been very polite when he joined them, but no; he was more quick-tempered than ever. He was not fond of young Turkeys, and their constant chattering annoyed him. "Can't you find some way to keep those children quiet?" he would say, and made such a fuss that the Hen Turkeys called them aside and tried to amuse them for a while.

Hen Turkeys are most loving mothers, and in the early spring first one and then another had stolen away to lay and hatch her eggs. If a Hen Turkey wanted a chance to lay an egg at this season, she watched the Gobbler and left the flock when his back was turned. As she came near her nest, she would stop and look around to make sure he did not see where it was. She knew that the Gobbler did not like to have her raise young Turkeys, and that if he could find the nest, he would break every egg in it. After she had laid her egg, she would wander back in a careless way, quite as though she had only been to the watering-trough for a drink.

Once the Hen Turkeys had talked about this when the Gobbler could not hear. "It doesn't seem right not to tell him," the youngest had said.

"Well, my dear," said another, "it is the only way we can do, if we want to save our eggs and raise our children. Gobblers always act in that way."

"Are you sure?" said the young Hen Turkey.

"Sure!" was the answer. "You wouldn't be here to-day if your mother hadn't done as we do."

So the youngest Hen Turkey had changed her mind and hidden her eggs like the rest, for, in spite of aching legs and all that is hard in hatching eggs, Hen Turkeys always want to raise broods in the springtime. When one of them had laid as many eggs as she wanted to hatch, she began sitting on them, and would not walk with the flock at all. One by one the Hen Turkeys had done this until the Gobbler was left quite alone. He did not like it at all, and wanted more than ever to find and break the eggs. When the Turkey Chicks were hatched, their mothers kept them out of the Gobbler's way, because, you know, he did not like small children and it was better that they should not meet.

The Hen Turkeys were very sorry for him, and often wished that he might watch with them the growth of their piping darlings, to see the tiny feathers push their way through the down and broaden and lengthen until there was no down to be seen—only feathers. It was too bad; yet that was the way in all Turkey families, and the Gobblers couldn't help disliking the children any more than the Hen Turkeys could help wanting to sit in the springtime.

By another year the Gobbler would love the young Turkeys dearly. Even now he did not try to strike them, as he might have done a while before. They were afraid of him, yet down in their hearts the brothers all thought that when they were grown up they wanted to be just like him and strut around with their wings trailing, their tails spread, their necks drawn back, and their feathers ruffled. Then, they thought, when other people came near them, they would puff and gobble and cry, "Get out of my way!" They tried it once in a while to see how it would seem, but they were still slender and their voices were not yet deep enough. The sisters laughed at them when they did this, and that made them feel very uncomfortable. The long, limp red wattles that grew out between their eyes became redder and redder as they swung to and fro under their short, thick bills.

"Just wait," said one young fellow to another. "Just you wait until I am really grown up and strut before your sister next spring. I don't think she will laugh at me then." And he comforted himself by eating fully twice as much grain as he should have done.

The farmer's little girl came into the farmyard, and all the fowls stopped eating to look at her. She was so young that she had never before been out there alone. Her father had brought her in his arms, and she had laughed with delight and clapped her little hands when the farmyard people passed by her. Now she had slipped out of the house and stood in the sunshine smiling at every one. She came without a cap, and the wind blew her soft yellow curls around her rosy face. It fluttered her red dress, too, and the Gobbler saw it and became exceedingly angry.

"Red-red-red!" he cried. "Why in the world did she wear red? I hate it!" He stalked toward her in his most disagreeable way, and you could tell by the stiff brushing of his wing-tips on the ground that he was very angry. "Get away from here!" he cried. "This is my home and little girls can't wear red dresses when they visit me. Pffff! Get away!"

The little girl turned to run as the big Gobbler came puffing toward her. In her fright she stumbled and fell, and he hurried forward to strike her. The Black Spanish Cock began to ruffle his neck feathers and stretch his head forward. He did not mean to have their visitor treated so. He ran between the Gobbler's feet and they tumbled over together. The little girl picked herself up and hurried into the house.

If the Gobbler was angry before, he was much more so after his fall. "What do you mean, sir," he said, "by tripping me?"

"And what do you mean," said the Black Spanish Cock, "by knocking me over?"

"Pffff! You were under my feet."

"Erruuuu! You were over my head."

Now nobody had dared to disagree with the Gobbler in so long that he did not know what to make of it, and when the Shanghai Cock strolled over to help his friend, the Gobbler was fairly sputtering with rage. "Ah, Gobbler," said the Shanghai, "wonder what has become of the little girl? It was nice of her to come out here, and I wish she had stayed longer."

"I told her to get away," was the answer. "She had on a red dress. I chased her. I always have chased anybody who wore red, and I always shall. It's my way."

"Is it your way, too, to be cross whenever you feel like it?"

"Of course. I wouldn't be cross when I didn't feel like it," answered the Gobbler.

"Some of us are not cross when we do feel like it," said the Dorking Cock. "I am always happier for keeping my temper when I can."

"Pffff!" said the Gobbler. "That is not my way. I say right out what I think, and then I am all right again and forget all about it."

"Humph!" said the Bantam Hen. "I wonder if the other people forget as soon? It would do him more good to remember it and feel sorry. He needs a lesson." Then she stalked up to him, looking as brave as you please, although she was really quite frightened. "I never noticed it before," she cackled, "but the tuft of hairy feathers on your breast is dreadfully ragged. And what very ugly looking feet you have! If I were going to have any webs between my toes I should want good big ones like those of the Ducks and Geese, not snippy little halfway webs like yours. I hope you don't mind my speaking of it. I always say what I think. It's just my way, and I never remember it afterward." She gave a graceful flutter and a queer little squawk, and was off before the Gobbler got over his surprise.

Fowls do enjoy a joke, and now the Dorking Cock took his turn. "I've always wanted to know how you spread your

tail in that fashion. It's a good time to see." He walked up beside the Gobbler and pecked and pulled until three feathers lay on the ground. "Ah," said the Dorking Cock, "I see I loosened some of your tail feathers. I hope you don't mind. It is just my way, when I want to know about anything, to find out as soon as I can."

And so one fowl after another teased and troubled the Gobbler, and explained afterward that "it was just their way." Then they laughed at him and ran off.

It would be nice if one could say that the Gobbler never again lost his temper, but he did, a great many times, for he should have begun to master it when he was a Chick. But one can tell truly that he never again excused his crossness by saying that "it was only his way." The youngest Duckling in the poultry-yard had always known that this was no excuse at all, and that if people have disagreeable habits which make others unhappy, it is something of which they should be much ashamed.

THE BRAGGING PEACOCK

THE farmyard people will never forget the coming of the Peacock; or rather they will never forget the first day that he spent with them. He came in the evening after all the fowls had gone to roost, and their four-legged friends were dozing comfortably in meadow and pasture corners, so nobody saw him until the next morning.

You can imagine how surprised they were when a beautiful great fowl of greenish-blue strutted across the yard, holding his head well in the air and dragging his splendid train behind him. The fowls were just starting out for their daily walks, and they stopped and held one foot in the air, and stared and stared and stared. They did not mean to be rude, but they were so very much surprised that they did not think what they were doing. Most of them thought they were asleep and dreaming, and the dream was such a beautiful one that they did not want to move and break it off. They had never seen a Peacock and did not even know that there was such a fowl.

A Lamb by the pasture fence called to his mother. "Ba-baa!" cried he. "One of the cloud-birds is walking in the farmyard." He was thinking of the night of the storm, when all the Sheep and Lambs huddled together in the meadow and watched the clouds, and thought that they were birds and dropped shining worms from their beaks.

Then the Peacock, who understood the Sheep language perfectly, said, "Paon! I am no cloud-bird. I am a Peacock." He said this in a very haughty way, as though to be a Peacock were the grandest thing in the world, far better than having one's home in the sky and bringing showers to refresh the thirsty earth-people.

The Turkey Gobbler never could stand it to have others speak in that way when he was around, so he thought he would show the newcomer how important he was. He drew up his neck and puffed out his chest; he pulled his skin muscles by thinking about them, and that made his feathers stand on end; next he dropped his wings until their tips touched the ground; then he slowly spread his tail. "Pffff!" said he. "I am no Peacock. I am a Turkey Gobbler."

The Hen Turkeys looked at each other with much pride. They were a little afraid of him themselves, but they liked to have him show the newcomer that Turkeys are important people. Their children looked at each other and murmured, "Isn't the Gobbler fine though? Guess the Peacock will wish now that he hadn't put on airs."

But the Peacock did not seem to feel at all sorry. He stood and looked at them all without saying a word, and they all wondered what he was thinking. Then a Duckling who stood near him exclaimed, "Look at his train! Oh, look at his train!" Everybody looked and saw all those beautiful long feathers rising into the air. Up and up they went, and spreading as they rose, until there was a wonderful great circle of them back of his body and reaching far above his head. The Gobbler's spread tail looked as small beside this as a Dove's egg would beside that of a Goose.

"Paon!" said the Peacock. "I am no Turkey Gobbler. I am a Peacock."

"Pffff!" said the Gobbler. Then he turned to the Hen Turkeys. "My dears," he said, "I think it is time that we walked along. The children should not be allowed to see and speak with any stray fowl that comes along. We cannot be too particular about that." Then he stalked off, with the meek Hen Turkeys following and the children lagging behind. They did so want to stay and see the Peacock, and they thought the Ducklings and Goslings were much luckier than they.

The Geese were delighted with the newcomer, and hoped he would be quite friendly with them. They wished he were a swimmer, but of course they could tell with one look that he was not. He did not have the trim, boat-shaped body that swimmers have, and then, his feet were not webbed. The Gander noticed that they were remarkably homely feet. He thought he would remember this and speak of it to the Geese some time when they were praising the Peacock's train.

The Drake was the first to speak politely to the Peacock. "We are glad to meet you, sir," he said. "Will you be with us long?"

"Thank you," answered the Peacock. "I have come to stay."

"We hope you will like it here. I'm sorry to see you do not swim. We should be very glad of your company if you did. You will excuse us if we go on to the brook. We are late already." He and all of his family waddled away to the water. "A fine-looking fellow," said he heartily. "Even my cousins, the Mallard Ducks, have not such a beautiful sheen on their neck feathers." The Drake was a kind, warm-hearted fellow, and it never troubled him to know that other people were handsomer than he.

The Geese were eager to reach the water, too, but they could not leave without asking one question. First they told the Gander to ask it, but he replied that if they wanted to know, they should ask it for themselves. Then they hung back and said to each other, "You ask him. I can't." At last the Gray Goose stepped forward, saying, "Excuse us, sir. You said that you were to stay with us, and we wish to know if you work for your living."

"I work!" cried he. "Paon! Never. The farmer invited me here to be beautiful, that is all."

"We are so glad," cackled the Geese, and the Gander joined with them. "So many of the people here work. They are very good, but not at all genteel, you understand."

"And don't you do anything?" asked the Peacock. "I thought Geese grew feathers for beds and pillows. It seems to me you look rather ragged. Haven't you been plucked?"

This was very embarrassing to the Geese. "Why, yes," they said, "we do let the farmer's wife have some feathers once in a while, when the weather is warm, but that is very different from really working, you know."

"Perhaps," said the Peacock. "If they want any of my feathers, they can wait until I moult. Then you will see how much they think of me, for whenever they find one of my train feathers (not tail, if you please; every bird has a tail, but I have a train) they carry it carefully into the house to be made into a duster for the parlor. I never give away any but my cast-off plumage. I am so very, very beautiful that I do not have to work."

This impressed the Geese very much. "We are glad to know you. Quite honored, we assure you!"

The Peacock bowed his crested head, and they bowed their uncrested and very silly ones, and then they went to the river. The Peacock thought them most agreeable, because they admired him, and they thought him the best sort of acquaintance, because he didn't work. It was all very foolish, but there are always foolish people in the world, you know, and it is much better to be amused by it and a little sorry for them, than for us to lose our tempers and become cross about it. That was the way the Shanghais, Black Spanish, Dorking, and Bantam fowls felt. They were polite enough to the newcomer, but they did not run after him. The Chickens used to laugh when the Peacock uttered his cry of "Paon! Paon!" His voice was harsh and disagreeable, and it did seem so funny to hear such dreadful sounds coming from such a lovely throat.

The Black Spanish Cock reproved the Chickens sharply for this. "It is very rude," said he, "to laugh at people for things they cannot help. How would you like to have a Lamb follow you around and bleat, 'Look at that Chicken! He has only two legs! Hello, little two-legs; how can you walk?' It is just as bad for you to laugh at his harsh voice, because he cannot help it. If he should say foolish and silly things, you might laugh, because he could help that if he tried. Don't ever again let me hear you laughing when he is just saying 'Paon.'"

The Chickens minded the Black Spanish Cock, for they knew he was right and that he did not do rude things himself. They remembered everything he said, too.

One day the Peacock was standing on the fence alone. He did this most of the time. He usually stood with his back to the farmyard, so that people who passed could see his train but not his feet. A party of young fowls of all families came along. Their mothers had let them go off by themselves, and they stopped to look at the Peacock.

"I do think you have the most beautiful tail, sir," said a Duckling, giving her own little pointed one a sideways shake as she spoke.

"Please call it my train," said the Peacock. "It is beautiful and I am very proud of it. Not every fowl can grow such a train as that."

"Oh, dear, no!" giggled a jolly little Bantam Chicken. "I'd grow one in a minute if I could."

This made all the other young fowls laugh, for they thought how funny the little brown Bantam would look dragging around a great mass of feathers like that.

The Peacock did not even smile. He never understood a joke anyway. He was always so busy thinking about himself that he couldn't see the point. Now he cleared his throat and spoke to the Bantam Chicken.

"I hope you don't think that I grew my train in a minute," said he. "It took me a long, long time, although I kept all the feathers going at once."

"Look at his crest!" exclaimed one young Turkey in his piping voice.

The Peacock turned his head so that they could see it more plainly. "That is a crest to be proud of," he said. "I have never seen a finer one myself. Have you noticed the beauty of my neck?"

"Charming!" "Wonderful!" "Beautiful!" exclaimed the young fowls. Just then one of the spoiled Dove children flew down from the barn roof and sat beside the Peacock.

"What homely feet you have!" this Squab exclaimed. "Are you not dreadfully ashamed of them?"

The young fowls thought this rude. Not one of them would have said it. The Peacock became very angry. "I know my feet are not so handsome as they might be," he said, "but that is no reason why I should be ashamed of them. I couldn't help having that kind of feet. They run in my family. I don't feel ashamed of things I can't help."

The young fowls felt so uncomfortable after this that they walked away, and the Squab flew back to the Dove-cote. For a time nobody spoke. Then a Gosling, who had heard her mother talk about the Peacock, said, "I should think he would be proud of his train, and his crest, and his neck, and—and everything!"

"Everything except his feet," giggled the Bantam Chicken, "and you know he couldn't help having them."

"I wonder if he could help having his train, and his crest, and his neck, and—and everything?" said a young Turkey.

They all stopped where they were. "We never thought of that!" they cried. "We never thought of that!"

"Let's go and ask the Blind Horse," said a Duckling. "He is a good friend of mine, and he knows almost everything."

They stalked and waddled over to the Blind Horse, and the Duckling told him what was puzzling them. The Blind Horse laughed very heartily. "So the Peacock is proud of having grown such a fine train and crest, but he isn't ashamed of his homely feet, because he couldn't help having those! There is no reason for either pride or shame with the Peacock. He has just such a body as was given him, and he couldn't make one feather grow differently if he tried."

"I don't see what anybody can be proud of, then," said a Gosling sadly; for, you see, she wanted to be proud of something.

"Be proud of what you have done yourself," said the Blind Horse gently. "Be proud of keeping clean, or of telling the truth, or of speaking pleasantly when things go wrong. There are plenty of chances to be proud in a good way, if one must be proud."

THE DISCONTENTED GUINEA HEN

"Well," said the Gobbler, "I should like to know what next! Last spring it was the White Pig, when we had never had any but black and brown ones on the place. Next it was Ducks, because one of the farmer's boys wanted them. Then it was the Peacock, to please the farmer's wife. Now it is Guinea Fowls for the farmer's other son. Society isn't what it used to be here, and while some of the new people may be very pleasant, I must say that I preferred the good old quiet days."

"I think it is lovely," cackled the cheerful little Bantam Hen. "One hears so much of the world outside, and for people like myself, who stay at home, that is a good thing. Everybody loved the White Pig before she had been here two days, and my children are very fond of the Ducklings. I like to have them together, too, for after I had told them positively that my Chickens could not go in swimming, they stopped teasing and became most delightful playmates."

"What would you say about the Peacock?" asked the Shanghai Cock, who had never been friendly with him, although, to tell the truth, the Shanghai Cock was not so grumpy as he used to be.

"Er—er—well," said the Bantam Hen, who tried not to say unpleasant things about people unless she really had to, "he—he is certainly beautiful, although I can't say that I am fond of hearing him sing."

This made all the fowls laugh, even the Gobbler looking a little smiling around the beak on the side where his hanging wattle did not hide his face. When the Hen Turkeys on the smiling side saw that he was pleased, they began to smile too; and then the Hen Turkeys on the other side, who hadn't been sure that it was safe for them to do so, smiled also. And it did them all a great deal of good.

"I didn't see the Guinea Fowls," said one of the Geese. "We were swimming when they came. How do they look? Are they handsomely dressed? We shall not call upon them unless they are our kind of people." It was some time since their last plucking for the season, and the Geese were growing more airy every day now.

"They are really very peculiar," said the Black Spanish Hen, "and not at all common-looking. I should call them decidedly genteel." Here the Geese looked at each other and nodded. They were always talking about being genteel, although if you had asked them, they might not have been able to tell what they meant by the word. "They are shaped quite like small Hen Turkeys," added the Black Spanish Hen "and their feathers are a dark bluish-gray with round white spots all over them. They do not wear any feathers on top of their heads. When I saw the first one, I thought she must have lost hers in an accident, but after the others came up, I knew it must be the custom in their family."

"And they are shaped like us?" asked the Hen Turkeys all together. They were thinking that perhaps the Black Spanish Hen would call them genteel-looking also, but she didn't.

"Very much like you," she replied. "In fact, I think they said something about being related to your family, although

I am not sure. Do you remember, dear?" she said, turning to the Black Spanish Cock.

"Certainly," he answered. "The Guinea Hen with the orange-colored legs said that their family was related to both the Turkeys and the Peacocks, and that they were pleased to see members of those families here."

"Gobble-gobble-gobble," called the Gobbler to the Hen Turkeys. "You must call upon our relatives as soon as you can. I will go later. I always wait to find out more about strangers before calling. It is my way." He didn't stop to think that if everybody waited as long as he did, the strangers would be very lonely.

After this, they scattered to feed, and the Hen Turkeys and their children looked for the Guinea Fowls. "Listen," said one, "and we may hear them talking to each other." They stood still, with their heads well up and turned a little to one side. They heard a harsh voice saying, "Ca-mac! Ca-mac!" and as none of their old friends ever said "Ca-mac!" they knew at once that it was one of the newcomers. They walked around the corner of the Sheep-shed, and there found them, a Guinea Cock and two Guinea Hens. One of the Guinea Hens had orange-colored legs, while the others had dark grayish-brown ones.

"Good-morning," said the Hen Turkeys. "Are you the Guinea Fowls?"

"We are," said the one with the bright-colored legs, "and you are the Turkeys, are you not?"

"We are the Hen Turkeys," said they, "and these are our children. The Gobbler didn't feel that he could come with us this morning, but he will come later. He got very tired in Grasshopper season and is hardly over it yet."

"That is too bad," said the Guinea Cock politely. "We hope he will soon be better. It is a hard time for all Turkeys—so much running to and fro, besides the stretching of the neck whenever a Grasshopper comes near."

"Perhaps he overate somewhat," said one of the Hen Turkeys. "We were quite worried about him for a time. He slept so poorly and dreamed that he was being chased. He always has a good appetite, and you know how it is when there is so much food around. One cannot let it alone."

So they chatted on about one thing and another, and walked as they visited. The Guinea Fowls were more fussy and restless than the Turkeys, and even when they were speaking would run after some dainty bit of food that had just caught their eyes. Of course the Hen Turkeys said how glad they were to have the Guinea Fowls come there to live, and hoped that they would enjoy their new home. All of the farmyard people thought it a most delightful place.

"Oh, yes," cried the Guinea Hen with the bright-colored legs, "it is very pleasant, of course, but I wish you could see the farm we left."

"Why! Was it better than this?" asked the Turkey Chicks, crowding around her. They were so surprised that they forgot their mothers' telling them that if they came they must be very quiet, and making them all repeat together, "Little Turkeys should be seen and not heard."

"Better? My dears, it was not to be spoken of in the same breath. I understand that when one has always lived here, this may seem very nice, but when one has known better things, it is hard to be contented."

"Still, we shall be very happy here, I am sure," said the

other Guinea Hen, the one with the brown legs. "People all seem so bright and pleasant. I like it very much indeed."

"We are glad of that," said the Turkeys all together. "We really must be going. We fear we have stayed too long already. The Gobbler will wonder if we are never coming back. Good-morning."

As they walked off to look for him, one Hen Turkey said to another, "It must be hard to come here after living on that farm."

"Yes," was the answer, "I suppose that we don't really know what comfort is here."

When the Gobbler asked them about the Guinea Fowls, and how they were enjoying their new home, the Hen Turkeys sighed and answered, "Oh, as well as they can enjoy this farm, we suppose." The Gobbler was a little surprised by this reply, but he said nothing, and as he pecked at the corn which had just been spilled from the load the Oxen were drawing, he thought, "I wish we could have better corn to eat. This does not taste quite as it should."

When the Geese met the Guinea Fowls, they began to speak of the pleasure of living on such a fine farm. "Ah," said the Guinea Hen with the bright-colored legs, "how I wish you might see the one we left when we came here. It was so different."

The other Guinea Fowls looked uncomfortable when she spoke in this way, and stood first on one foot and then on the other. Then the Cock said something about the sunshiny fall weather, and the good neighbors, and—and—

The Gander spoke again of the farm. "It is not all that we could wish," said he; "still there are some good things about it. There are several swimming places which are fine and cold in winter."

"If it were only better cared for," said the Gray Goose. "I had a dreadful time a while ago, when I tried to get through a hole in the fence. I don't remember what was the matter with the hole, and perhaps I never knew, but the farmer should have such things fixed. My neck was lame for days afterward, and he was wholly to blame."

After this, the Geese found fault with almost everything, and when there was no one thing to grumble about, they sighed because, "It was so different from what it might be." It was not long before even the spring Chickens, the Goslings, and the Ducklings were speaking in the same way, and the poultry-yard was a most doleful place. The Bantam Hen was the only really cheerful fowl there, and she got so tired of hearing the rest sigh and grumble, that she often slipped between the pickets of the fence and went to have a comfortable chat with the Oxen.

One day she fluttered toward them in a most excited manner. "Do I look nearly crazy?" said she. "I feel so. Ever since our last storm, the Guinea Fowls have been shut in with us, and I would give half of my tail-feathers if they had never come here. That one with the orange-colored legs can't see good in anything, and all of our steady, sensible fowls have heard it until they begin to believe that this farm is a wretched place."

"What do they do?" asked the Nigh Ox, who always enjoyed hearing the Bantam Hen talk.

"Do?" said she, shaking her dainty little head. "They don't do much of anything. That is what is the matter, and the young fowls are the worst of all. You know how it used to be at feeding time? We all fluttered and squabbled for the first chance at the food. Some Hen got the biggest piece, and then the rest would chase her from one corner to another, and not give her a chance to break and swallow any of it until she would share with them. It was great fun, and we never left a scrap uneaten. Now, what do you think?"

"Can't imagine," exclaimed the Oxen in one breath.

"Well, they all stand around on one foot for a while, and I am the only one eating. Then somebody says, 'I wonder if this is any better than the last we had.' Another will groan, 'Oh, is it time to eat again?' or, 'Suppose I must eat something to keep up my strength.' Then I hear the bright-legged Guinea Hen say, 'Ca-mac! Ca-mac! This is all so different, so very different from what I have been used to.' The Cock and the other Hen of that family are nice enough if you only get them away from her."

"What nonsense!" exclaimed the Oxen together, and they spoke quite sharply for them.

"I wish," said the Bantam Hen very slowly, and as though she meant every word—"I wish the bright-legged one were back where it was 'so different.' Perhaps then my friends would begin to act like themselves."

"Where did she come from?" asked the Off Ox. "It seems to me that I saw a bright-legged Guinea Hen somewhere not long ago." He thought very hard, so hard that he swallowed his cud without knowing he did so.

"Wasn't it at the place where we took that load of stone the other day?" asked the Nigh Ox, trying to help his brother.

He knew how disagreeable it is not to be able to recall anything of that sort.

"It was," cried the Off Ox; "and a very poor farm it is. It was the same Hen too. Talk about its being different! I should say it was different from this place, but there are a good many ways of being different. Um-hum! I think I will talk with the discontented Guinea Hen before long, and I want you to see that the other fowls are listening when I do."

Although he would say nothing more, the Bantam Hen saw from the look in his eyes that he meant to stop the Guinea Hen's complaining, so she went away feeling happier. Then the Off Ox unswallowed his cud and began to chew it as though nothing had happened. His brother heard him chuckle once in a while, and say, "Different!" under his breath.

When the Off Ox awakened from time to time during that night and heard the Guinea Hens talking in the dark, he chuckled again to himself. The Guinea Cock was a sound sleeper, but the Hens always talked a great deal between sunset and sunrise, and especially if it were about to rain. Other people thought that they might talk more in the daytime and then keep quiet when their neighbors wanted to sleep. They declared that they always remembered so many things to say as soon as they went to roost, and that if they waited until morning they might forget more than half.

The very next day, the Off Ox had the chance he wanted. He and his brother were yoked to the stone-boat and left standing by the poultry-yard. "Good-afternoon," said he. "Is the bright-legged Guinea Hen here?"

"I am," she answered, coming close to the pickets.

"We are just going over to your old home," said he, "with

this load of stone. Have you any messages to send to your friends?"

The Guinea Hen looked rather uncomfortable, and stood first on one foot and then the other. "Tell them I am well," said she.

"I will," said the Off Ox, in his hearty way. "I will try to tell them all. I think I can, too, for there did not seem to be many people in that farmyard. I didn't see Ducks or Geese at all. Are there any living there?"

"No," said the Guinea Hen. She did not seem to think of anything else to say, although nobody spoke for a long time.

"Of course not!" exclaimed the Off Ox. "How stupid of me to ask. There is no brook or river on that farm."

Still the Guinea Hen said nothing.

"We are dragging stone for their new barn," said the Off Ox. "Or perhaps I should say for their barn. One could hardly say that they have any yet, although I suppose they use those loosely built sheds for barns. I wonder people can spend a winter where there are such drafts; still, home is always home, and people love it for that reason. We are glad to have your family with us, not only to keep away the Crows (which was part of the Guinea Fowls' work), but because you will be more comfortable. I've never yet in all my travels seen so good a farm as this, and the one you left was so different! Good-bye."

There was not much talking in the poultry-yard the rest of the afternoon, although most of the fowls looked happier than they had for many days. When supper-time came, the Dorking Hen snatched the biggest pieces of food, and the others chased her from corner to corner in quite the old way. Every scrap was eaten, and nobody laughed when the Shanghai Cock said that the fine weather had given him a better appetite. It was really a dark and chilly day, but they had stopped thinking how much better off they would be if they only lived somewhere else. As soon as they stopped thinking that, they could see how well they were cared for at home. And so, although nobody had really looked at the sky or thought about the weather, everybody had a feeling that the sun must have been shining.

Perhaps the Guinea Cock and the other Guinea Hen were the happiest of all, for they had not known what to do or say when the bright-legged one talked about her old home. It all seemed like a joke now, yet she never liked the Off Ox after that day. The other fowls were as nice to her as ever, for they knew it was a sad thing to be so discontented, and they knew, also, that if they had not been foolish enough to let her, she could never have made them unhappy.

THE OXEN TALK WITH THE CALVES

It was a clear, cold winter morning, and the Cattle stood in the barnyard where the great yellow straw-stacks were. They had nibbled away at the lower part of these stacks until there was a sheltered place underneath. The Calves liked to stand on the sunshiny side with an over-hanging ledge of straw above their heads. The wind did not strike them here, and they could reach up and pull out wisps to eat when they had nothing else to do. Not that they were so fond of eating straw, but it was fun to pull it out. There was, however, usually something else to be done, for there was always their cud to chew.

Among all the farmyard people, there were none more particular about their food. They might eat in a hurry when time was short, or when the grass was fresh and green, but after they had swallowed it and filled the first of their four stomachs with partly chewed food, they would find some quiet and comfortable place where they could stand or lie easily and finish their eating. To do this, they had to bring the partly chewed food from the first stomach to the mouth again. They called this "unswallowing it," although they should have said "regurgitating."

After the food was back in their mouths again, it was spoken of as their cud, and the stout muscles in the sides of their faces pulled their lower jaws up and down and sideways, and the food was caught over and over again between the blunt grinding teeth in the back part of their mouths, and was crushed, squeezed, and turned until it was fine, soft, and ready to swallow into the second stomach.

Then the Cattle do not have to think of it again, but while they are doing something quite different, and perhaps forgetting all about it, there are many nerves and muscles and fine red blood-drops as busy as can be, passing it into the third and fourth stomachs, and changing the strength of the food into the strength of the Cattle. The Cows and the Oxen do not know this. They never heard of muscles and nerves, and perhaps you never did before, yet these are wonderful little helpers and good friends if one is kind to them. All that Cattle know about eating is that they must have clean food, that they must eat because they are hungry and not just because it tastes good, and that they must chew it very carefully. And if they do these things as they should, they are quite sure to be well and comfortable.

The Oxen were standing by the barn door, and the Calves were talking about them. They liked their uncles, the Oxen, very much, but like many other Calves the world over, they thought them rather slow and old-fashioned. Now the Colts had been saying the same thing, and so these half-dozen shaggy youngsters, who hadn't a sign of a horn, were telling what they would do if they were Oxen. Sometimes they spoke more loudly than they meant to, and the Oxen heard them, but they did not know this.

"If I were an Ox," said one, "I wouldn't stand still and let the farmer put that heavy yoke on my neck. I'd edge away and kick."

"Tell you what I'd do," said another. "I'd stand right still when he tried to make me go, and I wouldn't stir until I got ready."

"I wouldn't do that," said a third. "I'd run away and upset the stone in a ditch. I don't think it's fair to always make them pull the heavy loads while the Horses have all the fun of taking the farmer to town and drawing the binder and all the other wonderful machines."

"Isn't it too bad that you are not Oxen?" said a deep voice behind them. The Calves jumped, and there was the Off Ox close to them. He was so near that you could not have set a Chicken coop between him and them, and he had heard every word. The Calves did not know where to look or what to say, for they had not been speaking very politely. The one who had just spoken wanted to act easy and as though he did not care, so he raised one hind hoof to scratch his ear, and gave his brushy tail a toss over one flank. "Oh, I don't know," said he.

"I used to talk in just that way when I was a Calf," said the Off Ox, with a twinkle in his large brown eyes. "All Calves think they'll do wonders when they're grown."

"I know I thought so," said the Nigh Ox, who had followed his brother.

"Well, if you wanted to," asked the Red Calf, "why don't you do those things now?" The others wondered how he dared to ask such a question.

"It doesn't pay," said the Nigh Ox. "Do all your frisking in playtime. I like fun as well as anybody, yet when our yoke is taken from its peg, I say business is business and the closer we stick to it the better. I knew a sitting Hen once who wanted to see everything that happened. She was always running out to see somebody or other, and sometimes she stayed longer than she meant to. I told her she'd better stick to her nest, and she said she didn't believe in working all the time."

"How soon did her Chickens hatch?" asked the Calves all together.

"Never did hatch, of course," chuckled the Nigh Ox. "She fooled herself into thinking she was working, and she made a great fuss about her legs aching and her giving up society, but she couldn't fool that nestful of eggs. They had gotten cold and they knew it, and not one of them would hatch."

"Wasn't she ashamed then?" asked the Calves.

"Didn't act so," snorted the Nigh Ox. "Went around talking about her great disappointment, and said she couldn't see why the other Hens had so much better luck."

The Off Ox chuckled. "He told her that he guessed it might have been something besides bad luck, and that the next time she'd better stay on her nest more. Then she asked him how many broods of Chickens he had hatched. Ho-ho-ho!"

Everybody laughed, and the Calves wondered how the Nigh Ox could think of it without being angry. "It wouldn't pay to be angry," he said. "What's the use of wasting a fine great Ox temper on a poor little Hen rudeness?"

This made them think. They remembered how cross and hot and uncomfortable they often became over very small things that bothered them, and they began to think that perhaps even Calf tempers were worth caring for.

At last the Black Calf, the prettiest one in the yard, said,

"Do you like drawing that flat wagon which hasn't any wheels, and scrapes along in the dust?"

"The stone-boat?" asked the Off Ox. "We don't mind it. Never mind doing our kind of work. Wouldn't like to pull the binder with its shining knives and whirling arms, for whoever does that has to walk fast and make sudden turns and stops. Wouldn't like being hitched to the carriage to carry the farmer's family to town. Wouldn't like to take care of the Sheep, like Collie, or to grow feathers like the Geese—but we can draw stone-boats and all sorts of heavy loads, if we do say it."

The Red Calf, who was always running and kicking up his heels, said, "Oh, it's such slow work! I should think you'd feel that you would never reach the end of your journey."

"We don't think about that," answered the Nigh Ox. "It doesn't pay. We used to, though. I remember the time when I wished myself a Swallow, flying a mile a minute, instead of step-step-stepping my way through life. My mother was a sensible Cow, and wore the bell in our herd. She cured me of that foolishness. She told me that Swallows had to fly one wing-beat at a time, and that dinners had to be eaten one mouthful at a time, and that nothing really worth while could be done in a minute. She said that if we were forever thinking how much work we had to do and how tiresome it was, we'd never enjoy life, and we wouldn't live long either. Lazy Oxen never do. That's another thing which doesn't pay."

The Red Calf and the White Calf spoke together: "We will always be sensible. We will never lose our tempers. We will never be afraid to work. We will be fine and long-lived cattle."

"Might you not better say you will *try* to be sensible?" asked the Nigh Ox. "You know it is not always easy to do those things, and one has to begin over and over again."

"Oh, no," they answered. "We know what we can do."

"You might be mistaken," said the Oxen gently.

"I am never mistaken," said the Red Calf.

"Neither am I," said the White Calf.

"Well, good-morning," called the Oxen, as they moved off. "We are going to talk with our sisters, the Cows."

After they had gone, the pretty Black Calf spoke in her pleasant way: "It seems to me I shall be an old Cow before I can learn to be good and sensible like them, but I am going to try."

"Pooh!" said the Red Calf. "It is easy enough to be sensible if you want to be—as easy as eating."

"Yes," said the White Calf. "I shall never lose my temper again, now that I am sure it is foolish to do so."

"Dear me!" said the pretty Black Calf. "How strong and good you must be. I can only keep on trying."

"Pooh!" said the Red Calf again. Then he lowered his voice and spoke to her. "Move along," said he, "and let me stand beside you in the cubby while I chew my cud."

"Don't you do it," cried the White Calf. "I want that place myself."

"I guess not!" exclaimed the Red Calf. "I'll bunt you first."

"Bunt away, then," said the White Calf, "but I'll have that place."

"Oh, please don't fight!" exclaimed the Black Calf. "I'll let one of you have my corner."

"Don't you move," cried each of them. "I want to stand

by you." Then they lowered their heads and looked into each other's eyes. Next, they put their hard foreheads together, and pushed and pushed and pushed. Sometimes the Red Calf made the White Calf go backward, and sometimes it was the other way. Once in a while they stood still and rested. Then they began pushing again.

While they were quarrelling in this way, getting warmer and more angry all the time, and losing those very tempers which they had said they would always keep, a young Jersey had stepped into the cubby beside the Black Calf, and they were having a pleasant visit. "What are those fellows fighting about?" he asked.

The Black Calf smiled a funny little smile. "They are fighting," said she, "to see which one shall stand in the cubby with me and chew his cud."

The Jersey Calf was a shrewd young fellow of very good family. "Perhaps," said he, "I ought to stay and guard the place until it is decided who shall have it."

"I wish you would," said she.

And that was how it happened that the two Calves who lost their tempers had a cross, tiresome, and uncomfortable day, while another had the very corner which they wanted. When night came, they grumbled because the Jersey Calf had come out ahead of them, and they thought it very strange. But it was not strange, for the people who are quiet and good-natured always come out ahead in the end. And the people who are so very sure that it is easy to be good when they really want to, are just the very ones who sometimes do not want to when they should.

The Black Calf was right. The only way to be sensible and happy is to try and try and try, and it does pay.

CPSIA information can be obtained
at www.ICGtesting.com
Printed in the USA
JSHW031045131121
20335JS00002B/118